WHEN THE ONE
YOU LOVE IS
GONE

Praise for *When the One You Love Is Gone*

It is impossible to read these pages without being moved by the shining honesty, anger, wonder, and humor that radiate from this grief observed. Here is theology in the trenches, God's presence in the depths, waiting to be discovered anew. What Miles offers is what every grieving person needs—permission to let grief be what it will be, without expectations and without limits, hoping that the compost of loss may one day prove fertile soil for new life. The gifts of our beloved dead remain with us, imperishable, our cloud of witnesses.
—**Felicity Kelcourse**, Christian Theological Seminary, Indianapolis, Indiana

Rebekah Miles has done us a great favor by sharing her journey through loss and the subsequent grief that follows. Her discerning mind becomes our guide as we wrestle with our own grief. As she knows, it is an agonizing journey. Her guidance becomes ours.
—**Peter James Flamming**, Baptist Theological Seminary at Richmond and author of *Healing the Heartbreak of Grief*

I quickly identified with the grief experiences recounted by Rebekah Miles as I remembered the death of my mother. Grief is an ongoing process and I was especially helped by Dr. Miles's "Thanksgiving Therapy"—thankfulness, hugging, adoration (worship and prayer), nature, keeping positive, singing, and giving. I could not stop reading this captivating book once I started.
—**Tom Carter**, United Methodist Endorsing Agency, General Board of Higher Education and Ministry

The grief attached to losing someone we love is heartbreaking, and all of us want to avoid it. We know it to be a journey filled with memories, emotions, regrets, and lots of questions, some of which will always be unresolved. We also know that one day we will have to live with it, or live with it again. In the book *When the One You Love Is Gone*, the reader is privileged to join Rebekah Miles on her journey. Interwoven within her story are reflections of the elders, as they too have grappled with personal loss. Miles's authenticity, wisdom, and faith make this a must-read for all, as it challenges one to look at grief with a fresh perspective of faithful living.
—**Bruce Fenner**, United Methodist Endorsing Agency, General Board of Higher Education and Ministry

WHEN THE ONE YOU LOVE IS GONE

Rebekah L. Miles

ABINGDON PRESS
Nashville

WHEN THE ONE YOU LOVE IS GONE

Copyright © 2012 by Abingdon Press

All rights reserved.

This book is printed on acid-free paper.

Library of Congress Cataloging-in-Publication Data

Miles, Rebekah, 1960–
   When the one you love is gone / Rebekah Miles.
      p.   cm.
   Includes bibliographical references and index.
   ISBN 978-1-4267-4586-7 (trade pbk. : alk. paper)   1. Bereavement.   2. Loss
(Psychology)   3. Bereavement—Religious aspects.   I. Title.
   BF575.G7M5295   2012
248.8'66—dc23   2012007087

Scripture unless otherwise noted is from the New Revised Standard Version of the Bible, copyright 1989, Division of Christian Education of the National Council of the Churches of Christ in the United States of America. Used by permission. All rights reserved.

Scripture marked NIV is taken from the Holy Bible, NEW INTERNATIONAL VERSION®. Copyright © 1973, 1978, 1984 by International Bible Society. All rights reserved throughout the world. Used by permission of International Bible Society.

Scripture marked NCV is taken from the New Century Version®. Copyright © 2005 by Thomas Nelson, Inc. Used by permission. All rights reserved.

12 13 14 15 16 17 18 19 20 21—10 9 8 7 6 5 4 3 2 1

MANUFACTURED IN THE UNITED STATES OF AMERICA

For my family

Contents

Acknowledgments ix

Introduction
Field Notes for the Pilgrimage xi

Chapter 1
Early Days:
Wading Through Hell, Catching Glimpses of Glory 1

Chapter 2
Making Our Way Through Rough Terrain 23

Chapter 3
Finding Comfort and Hope in the Landscape of Grief 37

Chapter 4
Reintegrating the Dead: Bringing the Dead
Along with Us on the Journey 59

Chapter 5
Finding Hope, Moral Purpose, and Spiritual
Transformation in the Landscape of Grief 73

Notes 93

Acknowledgments

I t takes a village to write a book. I owe thanks to many people. I am grateful to Dean Lawrence and my colleagues at Southern Methodist University; to Bishop Crutchfield and my colleagues in The United Methodist Arkansas Conference; to Kathy Armistead and others at Abingdon Press; to the many friends from Facebook and CaringBridge who offered comfort in our grieving and encouragement in my writing; to the good members of First United Methodist in Fort Worth, Hot Springs, and Jonesboro and of Congregation Beth Israel in Asheville for their support; to the doctors and other health care professionals who cared for my mother in those final weeks; to the women with whom I pray—Karen Baker-Fletcher, Martha Brooks, Mitzi Ellington, Elaine Heath, Linda McDermott, Carol Montgomery, and Jeanne Stevenson-Moessner—and to the Luce Foundation and the Louisville Institute for giving me and so many others the gift of time to write.

I owe thanks to those who offered comments on the manuscript—Julie Mavity-Maddalena, Geoffrey Moore, Carolyn Douglas, Kathy Armistead, Carol Montgomery, Mireya Martinez, Dawn Weaks, Cornelia DeLee, Maxine Allen, Zetha Bone, Karen Huber, Denise Winslow, Mitzi Ellington, Linda McDermott, Jeanne Stevenson-Moessner, Stephanie

Ahlschwede, Mary Kemp, Pam Beeler, Cary Long, Stacey Piyakhun, Susan Gross, Jena Nelson, Ramsey Patton, Brenda Wideman, Jim Adler, plus family members Len Delony; Debi, John, Susan, Zoe, John, and Heather Miles; and Caleb, Josh, and Marc Rudow.

It may take a village to write a book, but, for me, it takes a family to grieve. I do not know how we would have gotten through this without one another. I give thanks for and to all the Mileses, Ridgways, Delonys, Rudows, and Vibhakars. I'm grateful to Uncle Mel and Aunt Kay for showing us how to grieve well through the terrible loss of a child and to Uncle Warren and Aunt Joy who saved my father's life. I give thanks for my sister, Deborah, and brother, John. I would have been lost without them. My husband, Len, and our daughters, Anna and Katherine, have seen the worst of my grief, and they love me still. My old father has shown us how to grieve and live well. My mother made this book possible, not so much by dying (which was terrible), but by making me promise, before she died, to write a book about it. It was the best thing for me. She knew what she was doing.

Grieving and book writing are not solitary activities. I have been fortunate to grieve and write in the good company of wonderful colleagues, friends, and family. I give thanks to God for them.

Field Notes
for the Pilgrimage

Great grief is a divine and terrible radiance which transfigures the wretched.
—Victor Hugo, Les Misérables

Grieving is hard. There is no getting around it. The bad news is that most of us never fully get over the loss of those we love; we bear those scars to the grave. The good news is that God is at work in us, turning our pain into something beautiful. I don't believe for a minute that God is in the business of zapping our loved ones and stealing them away from us. But in a world where death waits for every person, God stands ready. God stands ready to receive our dead; and God stands ready to guide us through the saddest days, to walk with us through our grief, and to take us into places we could never have imagined—places of hope and renewal. If God could take a cross and broken body and make of them redemption, then God can take our pain and heartache and fashion them into new life. Still, when the one you love is gone, you never fully get over it, and that, itself, can be a gift.

Grief Is a Beautiful Golden Ball,
Shining Like the Sun . . . Or Is It?

A few nights after my mother's death, I dreamed the words: "Grief is a beautiful golden ball, shining like the sun." In the dream, I looked up and there it was, an unspeakably beautiful sphere of light, radiant and pulsing.

In the months that followed, grief seemed anything but beautiful. It was messy—literally messy—with the tears, the snot, and the tissues. At my father's house, the bills piled up on the dining table, and by his carport door stood a tower of empty casserole dishes waiting to be returned to their owners. Our emotions were raw. We cried and raged over little things—a misplaced electric bill or a speeding ticket—because we could not bear to focus on the one big thing. Grief was messy.

Even though I did not fully believe it, I kept remembering that dream and wondering if it could be true that grief is, in the end, a beautiful golden ball, shining like the sun. Could our grief, in spite of all the evidence to the contrary, be a source of divine radiance, of light? I have written a lot about grief since our mother's death and have lately realized that all those pages are a record of my search for the beauty and value in grief. Our most difficult emotions can become, in the light of God's grace, a hothouse for the beautiful—for growth in compassion, an increase in faithfulness, and a commitment to make our lives more useful. The very emotions we are tempted to shun are the ones that may, by God's grace, bear the greatest fruit. God takes the poorest of materials and turns them into something holy.

Soon after writing about this dream of grief as "a beautiful golden ball," I woke up in a deep funk. I was ticked off. The image of the golden ball was rubbish. Grief is no shining, golden ball; it is a rank sinkhole. I had no more business looking for beauty in that sinkhole than in the underside of a stinking outhouse.

Both are true. Grief is a beautiful golden ball, shining like the sun, and grief is a rank sinkhole. To refuse either the golden ball or the rank sinkhole is to lose the gift. The way of our strange

God is not to get us into these messy places but to sit with us once we are there. Oddly enough, those difficult spots are the places our dear, peculiar God likes to frequent. Those are the very places God shows up bearing gifts—providing manna in a desert wilderness, bringing the Word incarnate to birth in a coarse stable, and offering God's own life to death on a cross. If God can do all that, God can surely help us in our grief.

Surprised by Ordinary Grief

When our daughters, Anna and Katherine, took their first wobbly steps, and then, again, when they began to stack a few words together in a fair imitation of a sentence, my husband, Len, and I were a mess of exclamation points. She walked!! She talked!! The most ordinary things in the world were, for reasons I never fully understood, occasions for amazement. The well-known fact that children across the world and through the ages had, in the normal course of things, learned to walk and talk did nothing to contain our gaping astonishment. She walked!

In December of 2008, my vibrant mother, JoAnn Ridgway Miles, had emergency surgery, and after a seven-week struggle in a small hospital in Hot Springs, Arkansas, she died. We prepared her body. We buried her in the hard ground. We mourned. My father, my older sister and brother, and I, along with a circle of family and friends, were a muddle of weepy exclamation points. She died! She is gone! This most ordinary of human experiences left us stunned. The sure fact, that across the world and through the ages, every last mortal creature has either already died or soon will did nothing to diminish our shock. She died! This book is about the most ordinary thing in the world: our grief in the face of a loved one's death.

Grief may be ordinary, but it is anything but predictable or routine. For years I have heard about Elisabeth Kübler-Ross's five stages experienced by the dying and the grieving: denial, anger, bargaining, depression, and acceptance. Knowing a little about this model of grief, I expected to pass through a series of stages and then, after some months or perhaps even a year or two, to move beyond those difficult emotions, letting go of my relationship with my mother and moving forward.

But grief surprised me; it has been nothing like I expected. I felt anger one hour and acceptance the next; then it was back to anger and on to regret with a bit of exhaustion and joy, gratitude and astonishment thrown in for good measure.

I began to wonder if I was doing something wrong. My mother had been moldering in the ground for a long time, but I was nowhere near getting over it. I was managing but still missed her, still talked to her, still thought about her everyday. I would have been really worried, except that the ongoing grief was not significantly hampering my life. If anything, grief had opened up my heart. I had greater compassion, stronger faith, and deeper bonds with my family. But I was still grieving.

Something was off. There were two possibilities. Either (1) I was failing the grieving process, or (2) I had some seriously screwed-up expectations about what that grieving process entailed. You have probably already guessed what it took me a very long time to determine. My expectations were, indeed, seriously screwed up.

Changing Models of Grief

In the last two decades, a lot has changed in the way grief is understood. A model of grief that emerged over the twentieth century and became popular in the 1970s and '80s offered what came to be a familiar story line.[1] A person in deep grief over the loss of a loved one is in an abnormal state. Although individuals grieve differently, there are typical patterns and experiences. By dealing with difficult memories and emotions that emerge after a loss, the person should, over time, be able to get beyond the painful emotions, let go of the deceased, and move forward toward new relationships and a new future. Failure in these tasks would be a sign of psychological pathology. That general story line endured for much of the twentieth century.

Over time, a new story line emerged to challenge the old.[2] After a death, people grieve in different ways depending on many factors, including the relationship with the dead; the circumstances of the death; the strength of the family; and the cultural heritage, gender, and temperament of the bereaved. More often than not, people grieve, not primarily as individuals, but within families and other communities. They may draw on an array of approaches to help in their grieving. Healthy grieving may follow a predictable pattern or be wildly unpredictable. Healthy grieving may be time-limited or lifelong. Confronting painful emotions will likely be called for, along with a fair share of avoidance. The goal is not to detach from the dead and let go of the painful emotions but to find healthy ways of living that allow the bereaved to deal with the practical changes in their lives, to continue their bond with the dead as appropriate, and, in many cases, to find moral and spiritual transformation. Grievers and their families and caregivers engage in an improvisational task of responding to loss. Grieving is creative; grievers make something of their loss. Grief in the face of death is not an abnormal, pathological condition to be cured but is an ordinary, albeit difficult, part of human life. My experiences of grief and my reflections in this book embody in many ways this new, more open-ended model.[3]

When I read about this new story line, my first thought was, "Hey, maybe I didn't flunk grieving after all!"—as if grief were a standardized test with scoring and assessment outcomes! Grief is not a test. There is no one right or wrong way to do this thing. That's good because it gives us some room and maybe even a little mercy for ourselves, but it also means we have to take responsibility for our own grieving.

The Pilgrimage of Grief

In light of this changing story line and my experience of grief, I have come to think of grief not as a condition with a series of stages and tasks that one moves through with the goal of finding resolution but as a pilgrimage. When we are grieving, we pass through difficult and tricky terrain—at times treacherous, at times beautiful. In intense grief we live in an in-between state, having left our ordinary world but not yet arrived at whatever new world awaits us. These times of transition, while difficult, are often rich with spiritual and moral possibilities. Although grief changes over time, for many grievers the pilgrimage of grief often becomes a lifelong journey that can shape their character, faith, and vocation in powerful ways.

My observations here are not a map or a set of instructions for the journey; these are my field notes, my observations of the terrain. Not everyone sees all of the things described in another person's field notes or sees them in a fixed order. Some people, because of cultural background or the context of loss, could run across some of the things described in the field notes more often than others, or some things not at all

Elisabeth Kübler-Ross acknowledged that grief was unique to each person. She once wrote, "Our grief is as individual as our lives."[4] If that is true, there may be as many different terrains of grief as there are people grieving. This book is based on my field notes, describing what I have encountered as I have wound my way through the rough and holy terrain of grief. It was written primarily for others who are bereaved. I hope that my notes will help you as you cross grief's uneven terrain.

Use It Up, Wear It Out:
Making Good Use of Death and Grief

Years ago, I was visiting my parents' house when I came upon my mother whistling as she sat at her beloved sewing machine. She was making little white zippered bags. I picked one up to look more closely and saw lettering on the sides, "Long Grain Rice with a Pleasing Aroma and Subtle Nutty Flavor." She was taking the seams out of empty cloth rice sacks and adding zippers in their place. I asked if it wouldn't be easier to buy some new bags at the dollar store. "But, Beka, then what would I do with those handy rice sacks? I can't very well throw them away—not perfectly good rice sacks!"

My mother hated to waste anything, from empty rice sacks to thin and patched bed sheets. She persuaded and bribed successive groups of grandchildren to memorize her favorite saying: "Use it up. Wear it out. Make do. Do without." As much pleasure as she took in the recitation of that line, she delighted even more in the performance of it.

Over the years our mother encouraged us not only to put old stuff to good use but also to find creative ways to make use of the refuse of our own lives: the bad things that had happened to us, the embarrassments, the losses. She brushed aside the question, "Why do bad things happen to good people?" and showed no

xvii

interest at all in asking, "Why do bad things happen to me?" She demanded an answer to a very different question: "What will we do with those bad things to make good things happen for us and others?"

I sometimes remind our young daughters of what Ma Ingalls would say in Little House on the Prairie books. In the wake of devastation of biblical magnitude—crop failure, pestilence, grasshopper invasion, flood, death, and famine—Ma would serenely remind her family, "There is no great loss without some small gain." That wasn't nearly good enough for our mother. Why let a great loss get by with yielding only a small gain? Let's milk that loss for all it's worth.

Now that I think about it, God, too, specializes in putting tragedy and destruction to good use. If the Bible is to be believed, God seems to operate on the same principle. God takes the shoddiest of materials—disobedience in a garden, enslavement in Egypt, and God's own death on a cross—and makes of them redemption. Really, the whole biblical narrative is just one big, divine cleanup operation after another—one extended exercise in creative domestic management. God knows how to keep house, even—maybe especially—when things are falling apart.

We knew our mother well, so I can't quite explain why we were surprised when she wouldn't hear of letting her own death go to waste. As she lay dying in the hospital, she used every form of weaponry in her maternal arsenal to wrest a promise from her children to make good use of her death. She was convinced that holes in the health-care system were one cause of her sudden plummet from excellent health to critical condition. She was furious and wanted her illness and death put to good use; organizing this task struck her as a fitting way to pass her last days.

As we stood around her hospital bed one morning, our mother began to orchestrate the responsibilities we were to take up after her death. Planning our life after her death seemed to cheer her immensely; we didn't have the heart to object. My sister, Deborah, a specialist in diversity education, was charged to create an exhibit "on the sorry state of our health-care system." Mom planned that my brother, a pastor, would preach a sermon on the evils of the health-care system. My brother, the Republican, and our mother, the Democrat, had so rarely agreed in the midst of life that it would have been untrue to form if they had suddenly agreed in the face of death. John tactfully declined. She knew better than to waste time trying to convince John, when she was, after all, short on time.

Mom then pointed at me. "*You*, Rebekah, will write a book about all of this." A book? My brother can get by without even preaching a fifteen-minute sermon, and I'm supposed to write a *book*! I made a counteroffer: an article for a church publication. On an ordinary day, an argument with my mother was a dicey proposition, but, at that point, the odds were, without doubt, against me. Though weakened in body, she carried enormous negotiating power; deathbeds will do that for you. She wanted the book.

The next morning, she was back at it. "I woke up from a dream last night with a good thought. I dreamed that if I die . . . and I probably will . . . it would be a more convincing book." She grinned. Evidently, the pain meds at this hospital were first rate; they made for happy patients. We wanted some too. "Listen. Mama, first, I did not promise to write that book. And second, you are *not* going to die." She grinned. "We'll see."

A few weeks later, when she was finally gone, we sent her body to Little Rock in the hope that there might be something left for somebody to use—maybe her corneas, we thought. But they shipped her back the next morning uncut; she had used it up and worn it out. There was nothing left to use in her body, but we were left with the task of how to use her death and our grief.

As my bereaved father says, "That's poor consolation, but we'll make do with what we've got."

An Open Book: A Note about the Text

Through those difficult weeks in the hospital and then for many months after my mother's death, I wrote a daily blog. It quickly became, in my parents' eyes, a ministry. My father, John Miles, is a retired United Methodist pastor, and my mother was an active laywoman. They saw most any occasion in life as an opportunity for ministry; that was the stained-glass lens through which they viewed their world.

I, however, am an ethicist and worry about little things like patient privacy. I felt compelled to ask my parents for permission before posting anything personal. I went to her hospital room one morning to ask if I could write about her negligible urine output and the next day to gain approval for a post on her rage at the health-care system. Mom finally told me, "Sweetheart, all these years we have lived as an open book. Whatever we have faced, if we thought it would help somebody, we talked about it. There is no point in stopping now. Write. Write about pee. Write about rage. Just stop bothering me with these questions!"

Much of this book is taken from what I wrote as our mother lay dying and especially in the months following her death; it bears the marks of my grief. The first chapter focuses on those powerful months immediately following my mother's death. I reflect on the strange emotions and thoughts of those days and try to make sense of them in light of my faith. The second chapter centers around typical hardships found in the terrain of grief. In the third chapter, I look at things that typically offer help and comfort to the grieving. In the fourth and fifth chapters, I write about the challenging tasks of reintegrating the dead into our lives and finding meaning and transformation in grief. Except for the first chapter, the book is arranged not chronologically but by themes. The effect is to make my grief seem more orderly than it actually was. Grief is, inevitably, a process of improvisational construction; our attempt to put order to the chaos of grief is, itself, a way to cope with grief.

These field notes on grief are less of a map than an invitation to those who grieve. Whatever shape your grief takes, I invite you think of grief as an *invitation to attention*. Attend to your suffering and to God's work within you. Simone Weil wrote of attention as the substance from which the love of God and neighbor are made. "The capacity to give one's attention to a sufferer is a very rare and difficult thing; it is almost a miracle; it *is* a miracle."[5] Giving one's attention to the sufferer is difficult, necessary, and miraculous, and it is no less so when the sufferer is one's self.

As we attend to our suffering and to God's presence within, we encounter a power in grief that will unsettle us. Grief may be a beautiful golden ball, shining like the sun, but grief is not all warmth and light and comfort. Victor Hugo described deep grief as "a divine and terrible radiance which transfigures the wretched." This transfiguration is never easy or comfortable. But by God's grace and power at work within us, our grief and our very lives can be transformed into something "abundantly far more than all we can ask or imagine" (Eph. 3:20).

CHAPTER 1

Early Days:
Wading Through Hell,
Catching Glimpses of Glory

Grieving is an altered state, especially in the days just after a death. It can be one of the most bizarre and difficult experiences of this life. If you are grieving now and you sometimes feel like you are going crazy, please know that it is temporary and normal. If it feels too hard to bear, please remember that over time it gets easier for most people. Whatever you are going through on your pilgrimage of grief, find help and support and always remember that the God who created you and your dead will suffer with you and sustain you.

There Is No Such Thing as an Individual

A few times over those seven weeks in the hospital, we thought we were about to lose Mom, but the world didn't actually shift until my sister called late that night on January 27 and said, "Beka, she's almost gone." Ever since that single breathtaking moment, the world has been "off" somehow. It isn't simply that the world before me is "a world minus Mom." It seems more sweeping than that.

The feeling is impossible to describe with any accuracy, but I have been thinking lately of those wretched animals thrown into a strange state before a storm. I have watched dogs pace and howl and hide under a porch; you can see them under there, crouched low with just their noses and front paws sticking out. They are uneasy in the world.

I am not hiding under porches . . . at least not yet . . . but I am uneasy in the world. Things are off center. It isn't just that the world has shifted; I seem to have shifted in some fundamental—though indescribable—way.

I have been thinking about D. W. Winnicott's astonishing claim that the infant doesn't exist as an individual but always as a relationship with the mother. He calls it the mother-infant dyad. Winnicott, a British pediatrician and psychoanalyst, once wrote, "There is no such thing as a baby." It's ridiculous, but somehow true, even so. Babies exist always in and as relationship with another.[1]

Maybe this is true not just of babies, but of everyone. We like to think of ourselves as individual units, but maybe there is no such thing as an individual in the way we ordinarily think about it. Maybe, at some level, our existence is made up of those bonds and connections with other people—maybe even with the dog hiding under the porch, maybe even with God.

Indeed, if Christians are right about God's nature, then God is relationship: the One made up of the three in communion with one another. This very God said, "Let us make humankind in our image" (Gen. 1:26). We, made in God's image, are then, by virtue of our creation and our creator, relational; we are not just made for relationship, but we exist as relationship. We are at our deepest nature, communal beings. There is no such thing as an individual.

If our very existence is bound up with the existence of those we love, then when those we love die, we die with them. We grieve then, not just for the dead, but for the parts of ourselves that are

2

lost. How do we keep moving forward after a part of us has died? How do we find our bearings in this unfamiliar world?

Where Are the Dead?

My sister, Deborah, keeps asking, "Where did Mama go?" and Dad wanders the house whispering, "JoAnn, my love, where are you?" She was here, and, then, in a moment, she was gone.

The simple, though not particularly satisfying, answer is that her body is in Hot Springs, Arkansas, about six feet under the earth at a cemetery near the corner of Hollywood and Shady Grove (which is precisely at 93.046303 degrees west longitude and 34.486538 degrees north latitude, if you want specifics). And her soul is with God . . . wherever that is.

Even though we know that Mom is more than her body—so that you cannot say, in truth, that she is near the corner of Hollywood and Shady Grove—what does it mean for people to be separate from their bodies when those dear bodies have been at the core of their identity and are necessary for our relationships to them? Put too crassly, what good is a relationship without a body?

Yesterday, we went with Dad to the grave, and he chatted away, telling Mom about the oatmeal we had for breakfast and the flowers in their yard. That's where widowers most often go to talk with their dead brides—to the graveyard. It seems peculiar to be standing with Dad as he talks to the air, but where else could he go but to the place where her body was laid?

This deep longing to connect with others as bodies is a fundamental piece of human existence. That's the manner of our knowing one other. We relate to the other not just with our bodies but as bodies.

For Christians, that's exactly why God came in Christ. The incarnation is all about God in a body. And now that I think about it, when God in Christ was embodied in the world, he spent most of his time dealing with bodies—healing sick bodies, raising dead bodies, and feeding hungry bodies. That's also what he called his followers to do—to tend to others by means of their bodies—clothing, feeding, binding, healing. We struggle to discern how we might continue the task of being Christ to the other when the other is no longer bodied.

It's Impossible for Mom to Die

If we had recordings of the rambling conversations among my siblings over the last few weeks since Mom died, the words *unbelievable* and *inconceivable* would be near the top of the word-frequency list—along with the words *Mother, death, lost keys, Dad, thank-you notes,* and *casseroles.* Just the juxtaposition of the words *our mother* and the word *dead* seems to go against what we evidently—and wrongly—felt was the natural order of things. How can the world keep spinning and the forsythia still bloom with our dear mother dead?

What a strange experience this is. It isn't just *sad* that Mom is dead; it is *inconceivable*. She can't be dead. It's not possible. And the certain truth that it is possible and that she is, in fact, dead, does not make it feel any less inconceivable.

In the early 1970s, our preschool cousins were loyal fans of Daniel Boone—not the real Daniel Boone, but the twentieth-century Fess Parker version they watched each afternoon on our living room TV. They were adamant that Boone was immortal; they would begin most conversations by jutting out their smooth chins and proclaiming, "Daniel Boone never died!" If you argued with them about the historical facts or tried to show them ency-clopedia articles with information about Boone's death, as their big sister, Heather, and I once foolishly did, things would esca-late. They would jump up and down, yelling, "Daniel Boone never died." We learned to humor them.

As ridiculous as it was, you could see an odd, internal logic behind this patently false claim. After all, how could something as ordinary as death take down the man described on their very own TV set as the "rippin'est, roarin'est, fightin'ist man the fron-tier ever knew." Every afternoon they had seen Boone face down bears and redcoats as well as historically inaccurate and offensive caricatures of armed native peoples; and Boone never died. He never even got winded! Death was simply not a possibility.

Some weeks before Mom's death, when things looked espe-cially grim, we were gathered as a family in the ICU waiting room talking openly for the first time about the real possibility that Mom might not make it. My sister went off on a rant, "People don't die of the problems Mother has." (This was patently false.) "Mother is not going to die. She can't die. It is impossible for Mother to die." (This, too, was patently false.) We looked at her and said nothing. Seeing the expressions on our faces, she stopped, took a deep breath, and then added defiantly, "And Daniel Boone never died!"

It isn't just that the idea of Mom's death seemed hard to bear; at some deep level it simply did not seem possible. How could Mom die? How could something as ordinary as death take down the mama, the creator, organizer, and sustainer of the family? For years she ate the right combination of crunchy orange vegetables and leafy green ones. She drank a gallon of spring water each day. Time and again Mom had faced down her children, her husband, assorted bishops, and state legislators; and she never died. She rarely even lost an argument. Death was simply not a possibility.

The fact that this claim was patently false did not make it any less emotionally compelling. Deep down, some little—or big—part of us believed that our mother could never die.

Looking Sideways at Death

Recently, I overheard our daughter Anna talking with a good friend and fellow fourth grader who lost her grandmother last spring. Anna told her, "I've decided to think that Mema didn't die. When I'm home in Texas, I'm going to think she is in Arkansas; and when I'm in Arkansas, I'm going to think she is still in the hospital and will come home later. I don't want her to be dead, so I'm going to think she is still alive."

Technically, Anna is not in denial. She knows that Mema is dead, but she has "decided to think" that she isn't dead, and she is explaining the details of her plan for pretending that Mema's not dead even when she knows good and well that Mema is, in fact, dead. When I mentioned Mom's death later that day, Anna scolded me, "Mom! Don't say that! You know I'm pretending Mema's not dead!"

I am amazed by the capacity of the mind to respond creatively in shock and grief. Dad has talked over the last few weeks about "looking sideways at death." He can't bear to face Mom's death head-on for more than a moment, so he notes death in his peripheral vision and then tries to focus his attention elsewhere for the sake of his sanity and survival. It's too painful to cast his full gaze upon it. The day of the memorial service, he told me, "Right now I'm looking sideways at death until I get my tasks done. Then I'll face it and walk that hard road."

The Drill Drills On: Suffering Is Unavoidable

It's Valentines Day, Dad's first without Mom. Last night was his first alone in the house since Mom died. Two weeks ago today, we gathered at their church to mark her passing. I look at the cheery calendar hanging on the wall of our bright kitchen and see month after month of cheerless anniversaries and sad firsts.

We keep coming up with new ways to help Dad: arranging trips, phoning him, asking other people to visit him. His sister Joy brings him strawberry milk shakes. When he was at our house this week, we served him blackberry cobbler with ice cream one night and apple pie another.

Still, Dad struggles. He wanders his house muttering to Mom and Jesus, and Jesus and Mom one after the other. "Oh, JoAnn, why did you leave me? Come back, my darling. Sweet Jesus, help me. Give me your peace, Lord. JoAnn, I'm lost without you. Help me, Lord." Dad tells us he is "wading through hell."

After C. S. Lewis's wife died, he wrote himself through that hell. In the middle of his journaling he asked, "Aren't all these notes the senseless writhings of a man who won't accept the fact that there is nothing we can do with suffering except to suffer it? . . . It doesn't really matter whether you grip the arms of a dentist's chair or let your hands lie in your lap. The drill drills on."[2]

I do not want Dad to suffer. I cannot bear to think of him at home by himself, crying for Mom. But, really, does it matter what I do not want or what I cannot bear? Regardless, our father is going to be at home by himself, missing Mom and crying for her. Strawberry milk shakes, phone calls, and even blackberry cobbler won't change that.

When we were living in Chicago years ago in an apartment building filled with other seminary students, a young woman—the wife of a student pastor from Korea—gave birth three months prematurely. The parents were told that their baby daughter had little chance of making it through the week. That first night after the birth, the father could say little without breaking down, so he said only this: "Dark tunnel; must go through."

I have often thought about that young family when I have witnessed others take that long forced march through hell. "Dark tunnel; must go through." No amount of phone calls or blackberry cobblers will change it. We still have to take that long forced march, just as countless others have before us . . . Christ included. Knowing that there is life on the other side does not take away the pain of the march. Dark tunnel; must go through. The drill drills on.

No Eye Is on the Sparrow

A few days after Christmas in 2003, Joan Didion and her husband, both writers, were at the hospital bedside of their daughter who had fallen into a coma. Later that evening, as they sat down to eat, her husband collapsed and died of a massive heart attack. "You sit down to dinner," wrote Didion, "and life as you know it ends." *The Year of Magical Thinking*, winner of the National Book Award, is Didion's account not only of the aftermath of her husband's death but also of her ongoing struggle as she cared for her daughter who died soon after the book was finished.

Toward the end of her memoir on grief and then, again, in its final sentence, Didion repeats a heartbreaking refrain: "No eye is on the sparrow."[3]

"No eye is on the sparrow." That is about the saddest line I have ever heard. I grew up with the old sentimental gospel song "His Eye Is on the Sparrow" and with the scripture on which this song draws: Jesus' insistence in Matthew 10 that as God is attentive to the sparrow that falls to the ground, so God is even more attentive to the individual person.

I have been astonished that faith has not lightened the grief. Perhaps faith will not save us from grief and sorrow, but I cannot imagine a world where "no eye is on the sparrow." And I have no idea how a person who sees the world that way could navigate life on ordinary days, much less on a day when "you sit down to dinner and life as you know it ends."

But however great the solace, trusting that God's eye is on the sparrow and on those we love does little to protect us from heartbreak. Faith does not save us from death, from grief, from loss.

Soon after our grandmother's death in 1990, my brother, John, was preaching a children's sermon using this Matthew 10 passage among others. With the children gathered around him, John talked about God's love for all of creation: "God cares for the lilies and the sparrows, and God cares for us too." His preschool daughter, Zoe, brought John up short, "But Daddy, don't you know? Lilies die and sparrows die and people die too."

God's eye is on the sparrow, but still the sparrow falls.

Faith does not promise that we will never have to walk through the valley of the shadow of death, only that God will be with us when we do.

Extraordinary Experiences

It is a joy to think that we will be with Mom again someday, but I would give anything to see her now, this side of eternity— just one glimpse. Last night I dreamed Dad and I were in a bus terminal, trying to figure out how to get to Mom; we were beside ourselves.

In the middle of her hospitalization, Mom came close to death and was resuscitated by her doctors. She appears to have seen her dead mother. It is common for the dying to say that they see their deceased loved ones. The living, too, often report that they hear or see their dead or feel their presence. In several studies of widows and widowers, approximately half said that they had had an experience of this kind. These experiences have been the subject of reputable studies to discern the effects on the bereaved. Known in the literature as Extraordinary Experiences or Post Death Contact (EEs or PDCs for short), they appear in many cases to offer solace and even to help the grieving deal with issues that were unresolved in their relationships with the dead.[4]

C. S. Lewis, after feeling the presence of his dead wife, acknowledged that the strength of the feeling did not constitute hard evidence about what actually happened. He then added, however: "If this was a throw-up from my unconscious, then my unconscious must be a far more interesting region than the depth psychologists have led me to expect."[5]

We have no way of knowing what really happens in these experiences. We can do little more than speculate. But I suppose that after a death, speculating on the extraordinary unknown is the most ordinary of human activities.

Radiant Dust

It is Ash Wednesday, my favorite day of the church year. You join a line of people walking to the altar where a pastor uses an ash-covered thumb to draw a cross on your forehead. If you are lucky, she will say, "Remember, O mortal, you are dust and to dust you shall return." It just doesn't get much better than that. Every now and then I come across a disappointing Ash Wednesday service during which the pastor doesn't really care for the death and dust theme and so decides to change it to a happier one. I think that's called Easter.

Five years ago, Ash Wednesday fell on what would have been my Grandmother Ridgway's 100th birthday. I remember the smallest detail of that service. I was standing in the aisle, when, out of nowhere, I heard my grandmother's voice addressing me. I didn't hear a voice externally but internally in a way that is different from ordinary daydreaming. The technical term is *internal locution,* and I am relieved to report that internal locutions are quite common within Christianity and many other religious traditions. That was a comfort at the time; if I was hallucinating, at least I was in good and heavily populated company.

My grandmother said, among other things, "From radiance you have come, and to radiance you shall return." I'm standing in the aisle thinking, "Whoa! This is not in the Ash Wednesday liturgy." But I didn't argue with her about it, because it was her birthday and she was one hundred . . . and also because she was dead! What's the protocol for that?

In retrospect, maybe I didn't argue with her because she spoke the truth. We human beings were made from the dust of the ground and divine breath. "God formed man from the dust of the ground, and breathed into his nostrils the breath of life" (Gen. 2:7). We are mortals in the image of God, formed from dirt and breath. We are radiant dust.

I'm not recommending a change in the Ash Wednesday liturgy, but ever since that day, when I go forward for the imposition of ashes, I remember that we were made from the dust of the ground and the breath of God. We are radiant dust, and to both radiance and dust we shall return.

Today I was at church enjoying the Ash Wednesday liturgy and got to thinking about my grandmother and mother, now together in eternity. Sitting there on a pew at the back of the church, I suddenly heard the clear alto voice of my dead mother behind me: "Glory. Glory. Glory. Rejoice." For one fine moment, I felt the glory, and I rejoiced.

It is fitting that as I was writing this reflection on radiance and dust, the toilet overflowed. I put the laptop down and picked up a plunger and then the mop. It isn't just dust and radiance that we are full of . . .

"Don't Know Nothin' 'bout Nothin'"

In 1842, Ralph Waldo Emerson lost his five-year-old son, Waldo, to scarlatina. Waldo died on January 27, the date of Mom's death. A few days later Emerson began journaling about his son's death and his own grief. He wrote, "Sorrow makes us all children again, —destroys all differences of intellect. The wisest knows nothing."[6]

Of all the things I have read about grief lately, those words ring the truest. As Dad likes to say lately, "We don't know nothin' 'bout nothin'." Maybe this is one of the greatest gifts of sorrow; it strips us of our ordinary confidence in our own knowledge. Grief doesn't render us dim-witted; it helps us see at last what was true all along. Oddly, there may be no more "advantageous" position for the spiritual life than knowing nothing.

This morning before school, the girls were yelling from the bathroom. They had spotted an armadillo digging in the dirt just outside the window. Len and I ran to the bathroom to watch this astonishingly dense armadillo shuffling around in the dead leaves and digging its little holes. If the window had been open, we could have touched it, but the armadillo did not notice us. We love armadillos, but they are stupid creatures. They have these tiny little heads and tiny brains without much room for activity. And, on top of that, their vision is lousy. There we all were with our faces pressed to the window just a few feet from this armadillo. But the armadillo noticed nothing. Nothing. Dense, stupid, near-senseless armadillo.

Maybe that's us with our tiny little brains and astonishingly poor vision. God and the saints and the angels and the heavenly hosts are just an arm's length away, close enough to touch. We see and hear nothing but just keep shuffling around in the leaves, digging our little holes. They look on, astonished that we could be so oblivious—and they love us still.

Losing Everything

Psychologists have written about two tasks essential to mature adulthood—working and loving. When we were camped out in the ICU waiting room, I began to wonder if there was another task of adulthood: the task of letting go. We spend so much of our lives working and loving. But the way the world is set up, if people live long enough, they begin to lose their loved ones, their work, and ultimately even their ability to work. The things of this beautiful world to which we have given our lives and our hearts are the very things we must let go.

I do not think God caused Mom's death, but I do believe that God has set up a world in which people, in the normal course of things, have to face the loss of those they love—including parents. This is a sad rite of passage and a part of our formation in faith. It's a universal experience of human life.

Involuntary Surrender

Recently, Anna, the family trickster, announced that she had decided to give up vegetables for Lent. Her father explained what she already knew: the point wasn't to give up something you don't like anyway. She put on her poker face, "Dad, people have to decide these things for themselves." The next evening, Anna refused the broccoli on the grounds of her Lenten fast. When we objected she told us, "Okay, I'll give up baths. Which do you prefer? Vegetables or baths?"

Lent is a good time to think about letting go. Of course, a lot of our letting go doesn't follow the model of Lent in which we choose what to give up. The hardest things to let go of are often the things we would never freely surrender. How do we faithfully let go of that which is taken from us?

Leo Tolstoy, in an 1856 letter to a much younger woman with whom he was in love, wrote, "One can live magnificently in this world, if one knows how to work and how to love." This quotation comes up a lot in scholarly and popular articles. But it is rare to find references to a companion statement from the same letter. Tolstoy tells his young sweetheart, "Ah if only you might learn, through suffering, to believe that the only possible happiness—true, eternal, elevated—is achieved through these three things: work, self-denial, and love."[7]

I wonder if self-denial covers enough ground. Our greatest losses include not just the things we freely give up but even more often the things we have not chosen—and would never choose—to give up freely. People don't choose to get pancreatic cancer or to watch their children die.

We do not choose these things, but we do have some choice in how we will respond to the suffering. After a loss, how do we respond faithfully? How do we join our suffering with the suffering of Christ and of Christ's body in the world?

14

Not Getting Over It

I have had it with letting go. It's overrated. It may not even be possible. I am beginning to suspect that you never get over this kind of thing.

C. S. Lewis, grieving his wife's death, wrote about the phrase *getting over it*:

> To say the patient is getting over it after an operation for appendicitis is one thing; after he's had his leg off it is quite another. . . . Presently he'll get back his strength and be able to stump about on his wooden leg. He has "got over it." But . . . he will always be a one-legged man.[8]

If we live long enough, we lose our sweethearts, our parents, our siblings, our best friends—sometimes even our children—and we go stumping about short a limb or an eye or a few fingers and toes here and there. The task isn't getting over it. The task is learning to live with our wounds. We may get around pretty well . . . for a person with one leg.

We often see our losses and wounds as negation. But maybe we have things backward. Disability theory is a new field exploring an ancient idea. The person with one leg or one eye is still whole, still fully human. Indeed, when our disabilities remind us of our vulnerability and necessary reliance on one another and God, they do not diminish but enhance our full humanity.[9] And, of course, even the healthiest among us are TAB—temporarily able-bodied.

The bereaved person is fully human not in spite of the loss but, in some strange way, because of it. Absence—whether of the limb or the eye or the beloved—somehow becomes, by the grace of God, a healing and holy presence.

This strange logic makes all the sense in the world in the light of our strange gospel. Christ reveals God's divine nature by emptying himself—coming into the world not just in human flesh but in the vulnerable form of an infant and then taking on the suffering of the world by giving himself over to suffering and death on a cross. This vulnerable God becomes our model for the Christian life. The "one-legged man," the bereaved spouse, the wounded mother on her deathbed, all participate by way of their wounds in the woundedness and vulnerability of Christ.

Grief as Presence, as a Bond with the Dead

In a novel entitled simply *Grief*, Andrew Holleran explores this language of "getting over" grief or "moving on." The main character is grieving after his mother's death. When someone tells him, "You have to move on," he replies, "But you don't . . . You don't have to move on." He describes the pull of grief: "Grief is what you have after someone you love dies. It's the only thing left of that person. . . . Your grief is their presence on earth."[10]

I pray that grief is not "the only thing left" of our dead, but I am struck by the way grief is not only an emotion of loss but also one of presence. Grief is a way of continuing the bond with the dead. Leaving the grief behind would itself be something to be mourned. In this sense, then, grief is not simply a wound or a deprivation but also a treasure and a presence, a connection with our beloved dead. Instead of grief being a process of letting go, maybe it's just the opposite. Grief is a time not of letting go but of finding new ways to maintain our tie with the dead.

We live in a world in which God intends for us to create these close bonds with others, and then, in the face of their deaths, we never get completely over it. That's the way things are. In our grief, we carry, tentatively, our bond to the dead. We limp along. And in the limping and the woundedness, we find our humanity. In our brokenness, we are driven to reliance on God and one another, including our dead. It's a strange world—strange and beautiful and sad.

Maundy Thursday/Good Friday: For Want of a Refreshment Table

It's Good Friday, a fitting day to think about death and grief. Dad is here in Fort Worth with us. Len asked Dad if he wanted to join him for Good Friday services at our church. "No thanks, son. I already know how it's gonna turn out."

Yep, we all know how it's gonna turn out. It won't be pretty, no prettier this year than the year before or the year before that. This is not a plotline that's likely to change from one Holy Week to the next, although that has been a topic of lively conversation in our house today.

Last night, we went to the Maundy Thursday service together. Near the end, we all processed silently out of the sanctuary to an adjoining garden, lit with torches for the occasion. One of our pastors read the passage about Jesus praying in the garden when the disciples fell asleep on him. As the congregation sang "I Come to the Garden Alone," Anna began jumping up as high as she could. I turned and asked her what on earth she thought she was doing, jumping up and down in the middle of the hymn. She said, "Mom, I'm looking for the refreshment table!" "There is *no* refreshment table, Anna." "No refreshment table?! No donuts?! No lemonade?!" Maundy Thursday was never a favorite of hers, but this was more than she could bear.

Ever since then, we have been hearing complaints about the

absence of the refreshment table in the church garden on Maundy Thursday evening. Dad told the girls that Jesus likely would have had a refreshment table if he had had the foresight to bring the women along—especially Martha. The girls began to speculate about what might have happened if there had been a refreshment table in the garden of Gethsemane. It would have been much nicer for everybody. The disciples wouldn't have fallen asleep if they had had donuts and lemonade, and when the Roman soldiers came, the disciples could have offered them snacks. As Anna observed, "It's hard to cut off somebody's ear when you're eating a donut." That is so true.

Katherine figured they needed snacks not just in the garden but the whole nightlong: "The people would yell, 'Crucify him, crucify him . . . Oh . . . Hey, are those donuts? May we have some?'" Then everyone would have had snacks together, and Jesus would have been all right—no crown of thorns, no cross, no tomb . . . no resurrection.

Geoffrey Moore, one of our PhD students in theology, on hearing this story, reminded me that there were, after all, refreshments provided on that Thursday night. It was called the Last Supper. Katherine knew intuitively what Jesus discerned long before. That if the community—the body—was to be torn apart, then that body would "need something to bring it back together, to nourish and sustain it over time." Jesus provided a meal—refreshments of bread and wine—that brought Christ's followers together then and brings us together now in his body. Through the breaking and sharing of his body, things are made "all right," not in spite of death, but through it.

Holy Saturday: Dead Bodies

It is Holy Saturday—the still point between the crucifixion on Friday and the resurrection on Sunday. To mark the day, I have been looking at paintings of Jesus in the tomb and ran across one that was unlike any other I had seen before: Hans Holbein's *Christ Entombed*. The Jesus of this painting looks so . . . dead. His face is gray; his mouth hangs open; his eyes are wide, in a fixed, empty stare. The painting is horizontal, on a long narrow canvas. We see Jesus as if he were enclosed in a narrow tomb, and we were viewing him from the side. His body is bruised. His wounds gape. It is a gruesome picture, repulsive frankly.

Somehow, when I have thought of Jesus and the passion, I have tended to skip straight from the cross to the empty tomb. It's easier that way. If I do think about the dead Jesus, something like Michelangelo's *Pietà* comes to mind; there is an elegant beauty to his limp form, the clean white marble, his features so delicate. That's my kind of death.

Holbein's *Christ* is in no way beautiful, in no way clean, in no way delicate. Here is a picture of Jesus that shows him as a corpse, a dead man, really truly dead.

A dead Jesus is even more scandalous than a dying one. Christians should be wearing little tombs around their necks instead of crosses. The astonishing thing isn't just that God in Christ was dying but that God in Christ was actually dead, entombed.

Really, that's a lot more shocking than the resurrection. After all, what is a little bodily resurrection for the Almighty? How hard could that be? But God dying? It's beyond comprehension.

The dead, entombed Jesus with his ashen face and open wounds takes on new power for me this Holy Saturday. Not quite ten weeks ago, in one of those private "visitation" rooms at the funeral home, I was standing with the women of my family by my mother's corpse, her really, truly dead body. She had asked for a simple burial—a plain wooden box, no embalming, no mortuary beauty treatments.

There her body lay, just as it had come from the hospital, just as *she* had come from the hospital, on a gurney with a sheet beneath her. She was in her skimpy hospital gown and still wore bandages.

Because she had died of an infection, or maybe just because she was dead, we were advised by the staff of the funeral home to put on rubber gloves to care for our mother's precious body. Our sister-in-law Susan brushed her hair, thin and grey in death as it had not been in life until the very end. Deborah took off the stained bandages and cleaned her wounds. We tried to remove the adhesive from her skin and to fix her body as best we could, but there was a limit to how much we could do. She was so battered—the incisions, the abrasions, the bruises. No amount of tending and care could change that heartbreaking fact.

As we cleaned her body, I remembered all the times she had cared for our bodies. These breasts provided our first food. These lips kissed our wounds. These stiff hands, once so warm and soft, had held ours through illness and night terrors. Now she lay there, her body shrunken, her hands stiff, her lips cold.

Earlier in the day, Katherine, with the help of her aunt, had picked out the burial clothes: underwear, a simple black skirt, a turquoise turtleneck, and a jacket. The sandals Katherine had picked out wouldn't stay on, so I took off my knee-high black boots and gave them to Mom—for keeps. Our twenty-year-old niece, Zoe, added makeup: a little blush, some lipstick. Mom's friend put on simple gold earrings. We decided she looked pretty good—for a dead person.

As we dressed our mother, I remembered a day nineteen years

earlier when my sister and I had stood with our mother by the corpse of her mother, dressing her for the last time, trying to get her stiff arms into the sleeves of the dress, working to get the panty hose slipped over her not-so-yielding legs. We sang hymns. We cried. We laughed.

As we prepared our mother's body, just as we had prepared our grandmother's those many years before, I was struck by how very dead they looked, really truly dead. In the weeks following my mother's death, I could not get the images of her sick body and her dead body out of my mind.

Holbein's *Christ*, ashen and entombed, is so powerful for me this year because I see now that long before my mother was wounded, long before she died and lay before us, an ashen corpse on a gurney, even long before she was born, God had come in human form and had taken on not only human life but also its woundedness and death in all its ugliness and brutality. Christ took on not just his own woundedness and death but my mother's as well. He took it on, not just for that time, but for our time and for all time.

The Resurrected Body

At the end of this Holy Week, I have been thinking not just about the wounded and dead body but about the resurrected one too. Christians have speculated for millennia about what the resurrected body will look like. Medieval paintings sometimes portray fields of bodies being resurrected from the grave in what was considered at the time to be an ideal form—that of vibrant young men without blemish or defect. The young men climbing out of graves are very beautiful, but it seems somehow obscene. What about the children and the women, the old people, and even the sagging middle-aged people like me? What about the bodies of the wounded and the infirm?

When the resurrected Christ appeared to his followers, he bore the wounds of the crucifixion in his resurrected body (John 20:19-29). Might it be true of the saints as well? Augustine, reflecting on the bodies of martyrs, wondered what would happen to their wounds at the resurrection. The "marks of the wounds," he wrote, "will add lustre to their appearance." These scars will be considered not blemishes but "marks of virtue."[11]

This Holy Week I wonder what will count as beautiful in eternity. The very wounds and defects that we consider ugly in this world may be marks of beauty in the resurrected body. Perhaps my mother's wounded body was beautiful in a way beyond our imagining. Her resurrected body may bear the marks of the wounds she took in this life, and those wounds may be her adornment, her beauty. Might the same be true of our grief? The wounds of the heart borne in this life may be our adornment in the next.

CHAPTER 2

Making Our Way Through Rough Terrain

Slogging through the terrain of grief may be one of the hardest things we will ever do. At times I wondered if there was something wrong with me; my body was tired and my emotions were all over the place. It helped to know that my experiences of grief, though difficult, were utterly normal. Whatever difficult things we feel—anger and relief, envy and gratitude, sluggishness and mania—it comes with the territory. Because the landscape of grief is so hard, we need to take care of ourselves and find whatever help we need along the way.

Effects of Grief

There are hundreds of lists of normal "symptoms" of grief. The bereaved can be distracted, withdrawn, and overwhelmed. They may have too little appetite or too much. They may have no energy one moment and manic energy the next. They may feel completely alone or suddenly find themselves infatuated with another person. Their stomachs and their muscles may hurt. They can have tightness in their chest, lumps in their throat, and aches all over. They may dream of the deceased, obsess about the deceased, rage against the deceased, or long for the deceased. They may feel guilt, anger, gratitude, and fear. They may sleep too much or too little. They may lose weight or gain it. In most cases, they weep. They cry out. They sigh.

It turns out that exhaustion is one of the most common symptoms of grief. Sleep disturbance almost always makes the list too. You would think that if grief exhausts us, then it would at least help us sleep better. But it doesn't work that way. I don't know when I have ever been so tired. Grief is not for the faint of heart or body. In Psalm 31:9 we read: "Be merciful to me, O Lord, for I am in distress; / my eyes grow weak with sorrow, / my soul and my body with grief" (NIV) Another translation reads, "My whole being is tired from grief" (NCV).

Embodying Grief

I never knew that grief was fixed so powerfully in the body. Grief isn't simply an emotional state; it has taken up residence in my flesh. The muscles in my shoulders and chest are tight. My hands are warm and sweaty in one moment and then cold and numb in another. My heart races. Sometimes, it's an effort to get a deep breath.

When we talk about grief, our words often reflect what we feel in our bodies. The word *grief* itself comes from the Latin word *grave*, meaning "heavy." The bereaved sometimes say, "I feel like I'm carrying a burden" or "the weight of the world is on me." After the last of her sisters died, our grandmother would sometimes tell us, "My heart is heavy." For years, I assumed that was just a figure of speech—one more way of saying she was lonesome for her sisters. But earlier today when I thought to myself, "My heart is heavy," it came to me: Oh, my heart really does feel heavy. There's a weight in my chest, but not just there. My arms and legs are heavy. It takes too much effort to wash the dishes or

heartache

take out the trash. So why bother? If grief is a kind of internal gravitational force, maybe I should just sit down. Dad says grieving is like "wading through molasses."

Some people use images of grief as pain or injury: "My heart aches"; "I'm broken hearted." The expression "to pine" for someone comes originally from an Old English word meaning "pain." Again, maybe people turn to these images because grief actually brings along with it physical pain and discomfort. The heart does feel broken; it aches.

The theme of absence is also common. You'll sometimes hear people say, "I feel empty," Or, "she left a hole that can't be filled." And sometimes there is a feeling of emptiness in the gut and chest, as if a big chunk of something inside has been wrenched away.

Each of these sets of images brings different feelings. The language we use to talk about grief both reflects and shapes our experiences of it—including how our bodies feel.

Grief Is Visible

The girls are learning to read my grief. Anna will sometimes say, "Mom, look at me." She comes close, holds my face in her hands, and examines it. Then she will announce, "Yep, she's fixin' to cry." Sometimes, she is wrong. And even if I *were* just about to cry, her examination makes me laugh. That's probably why she does it.

When Mom was in ICU, we had many opportunities to observe grieving faces and postures. When I went into the restroom of the ICU waiting area and saw my own face in a mirror, I was shocked by the grief etched there. I had no idea that I looked just like all those other worn-out family members.

I found this quotation about the expression of grief in the body. It is a description of a woman in mourning from Anthony Trollope's *Prime Minister*: "Her gown, and her cap, and her strings were weeping. Her voice wept, and her hair, and her nose, and her mouth."[1]

Humans are not the only ones who show physical signs of grief. Joyce Poole, who for many years has worked with elephants in a national park in Kenya, wrote of a mother elephant who kept "vigil" over her dead child: "I will never forget the expression on her face, her eyes, her mouth, the way she carried her ears, her head, and her body. Every part of her spelled grief."[2] Animals will howl over the dead body of a mate or child. Primates, dogs, and other animals will sometimes stop eating when a member of their community dies. Jane Goodall, the world's foremost authority on chimpanzees, describes young chimps that, on losing their mothers, showed behaviors much like human children in grief: "hunched posture, rocking, dull staring eyes, lack of interest in events around them."[3] In our sorrow we find solidarity not only with other humans who grieve but also with nonhuman creatures.

Why Grief: Evolutionary Psychology

Dad and I have both been sick lately. It turns out that grief is hard on our bodies. When men lose their wives, their chances of dying within the year increase significantly. Grief will kill you.

I have been reading a book on evolutionary psychology and grief.[4] The underlying question is simple: If grief is so hard on health and survival, then why is it such a strong impulse? Grief is a trade-off. It may not be good for us, but strong attachments are. It is a great benefit for humans to have deep desires for attachments and a strong impulse to seek reattachment in the event of separation. The pain of separation can be a goad to seek healing in the relationship. But when, by death, those bonds are broken beyond repair, the cost is high. The joy of attachments may far outweigh the pain of their rupture, but it's precisely because the joy is so great that the loss is so difficult to bear.

God, too, seeks to establish bonds of love and to strengthen those bonds when they are weakened. And it seems that God grieves when those bonds are broken. That is God's nature. As bearers of God's image, it is ours as well.

Greylag Goose, Calling Behavior

On those long lists of normal grieving behaviors, one of the more common is "searching and calling out." Many mourners find themselves oddly looking for and calling out to the dead person, even though they know perfectly well that the person is gone. In his book *Bereavement*, Colin Murray Parkes notes similar patterns in animals. The Greylag Goose, on losing its mate, will fly around searching in all the places where the mate might be found, crying over and over the same "penetrating trisyllabic long distance call."[5]

For a long time after Mom's death we found ourselves doing the same thing—without the flying, I'm sad to say. I would catch myself whispering, "Mama, Mama, Mama." Across the world, many children "call out" after a mother dies—even children who are well into middle age.

Lately, I have tried to shift that search-and-call pattern. It feels so sad to say, "Mama, Mama, Mama." Sometimes I consciously shift and say instead: "Thank you, Mama. Thank you, Mama. Thank you, Mama."

Grief and Anger: Tombstone

It turns out that intense anger is common among the bereaved, and, if my family is any indicator, rampant cussing appears to accompany that rise in anger. Dad was furious last night. The owner of the monument company had called to say that the cemetery association wouldn't approve the footstone Dad had ordered: a combined footstone for both of them. This would violate the cemetery rules. Each person must have his or her own separate footstone.

Dad was livid; he told me, "@#%&@, I don't want my own little footstone. If I wanted my own little footstone, I wouldn't have married that woman to begin with." Our dear elderly father claims he's ready "to go down there and whup somebody's butt." Because we know he would never do it, we all enjoy the empty threat. We are glad to hear the fire back in his voice.

Dad isn't the only one whose grief is being expressed in anger. My siblings and I have had a lot of anger about the medical circumstances that led to our mother's hospitalization. During the hospitalization and the early days after her death, our anger was often expressed in colorful accusations.

I have lost count of the times that one of us has said to the other or to our spouses, "That @#%&@ killed our mother." Or, "Those SOB bureaucrats who make decisions about Medicare killed our mother." But then we remind ourselves that our mother would object to that language. She didn't approve of linking the term SOB with bureaucrats; it was an insult to innocent female dogs and their male descendants. She preferred the phrase "son of a witch burner." We could live with that. "Those sons of a witch burner bureaucrats killed our mother." Grief brings out lots of strong emotions—including anger and even unreasonable anger. I have thought about anger as a negative side effect of grief, but maybe anger can, in some circumstances, be an antidote as well. It's just a part of our terrain of grief . . . cussing too.

The ICU Bandit: The Illusion of Control

I keep going in mental circles, thinking back over Mom's illness and hospitalization—the things we did, the things we didn't do. In the middle of the night, I stare at the ceiling and think, *If only we had done that test sooner. What if we had called this doctor instead of that one?* I've worn a path of questions, and no matter how often I pull myself away, I find myself right back on that same God-forsaken track. What if? What if? What if? If only . . . If only . . . If only. This is getting old.

Recently my husband, Len, found a note that Mom had written to him during that first week in the hospital. She thanked him for taking care of our daughters while I was in Hot Springs caring for her. She wrote that I had saved her life. I read that line as one miserable exclamation point to my failure. I bore it as an indictment. All the time she was sick, I kept thinking I could do something to save her. It turned out I was wrong; but, by God, I tried.

I tried so hard that my father began introducing me to the doctors as "my daughter, the Holy Terror." After Mom was in ICU, I tried all the harder . . . okay, maybe a little too hard. I loitered by the staff elevators near ICU so I could collar the nurses at shift change to ask about Mom. I camped in the hallway outside of the ICU doors where I could waylay the doctors to offer my eager, if inept, medical advice. By observing the ICU custodians, I even learned the door pass code so that I could sneak into ICU during off-hours and check things out. My family took to calling me "the ICU Bandit." Somehow, I thought if I were vigilant enough, Mom would be okay.

A friend talked with me several years ago about her teenage son, a drug addict who would disappear for months. She told me, "For the first year, I was terrified because I was no longer in control. Then I began to realize that I had never been in control. It was just easier to maintain the illusion when life happened to be going according to plan." Maybe deaths and debilitating illnesses reveal what was true all along: we aren't in control.

As much as I abhor not being in control, a small part of me remembers that it is often in these scary places—places where we are emptied of our ordinary illusions of control and our customary power—that God shows up bearing gifts that only empty hands can hold.

Envy and Irritation

Within those first weeks after Mom died, I kept running across sweet people who were caring for their elderly mothers . . . and I despised them. A friend sat down in a church pew beside his mother and put a sweater across her shoulders. In this tender moment, I was overcome by ferocious envy. Honestly, I wanted to whack him with a pew Bible. How could he have the good fortune to help his elderly mother when my mother was gone?

It turns out that irrational envy and bitterness are common feelings of the bereaved. There's nothing to do but notice it and try not to be too hard on ourselves. We might also do our best to be kind to these people whose only "fault" is that they are caring for their loved ones. Hitting them with a pew Bible, however tempting, is probably not a good idea. I'll have to restrain myself.

Speaking of irritations that come with the terrain of grief, what about the sweet people who say things that are meant in love but don't sound so loving? A kind friend smiled and patted me on the shoulder, "God had a purpose in taking your mother." Smile and pat. "It was God's will." Smile and pat. That's the kind of God I wouldn't even want to share a taxicab with. Other grievers may be bothered by different things people say, but the underlying irritation is shared. No matter how irritated we get, what can we say or do to these sweet people? We have already determined that violence by pew Bible is off the table. My ordinary strategy is simple: smile, pat, and run away.

Grieving Many Little Things

When Mom was eighteen and had been dating Dad for a few months, she invited him to meet her parents and little brother, Mel, at their home in east Arkansas. Dad brought asters as a gift for her mother. When our Grandmother Ridgway opened the door, Dad gave her the asters, and she broke down in tears. A few months earlier, her mother had died. Asters were her mother's favorite flowers, and the sight of them brought on a wave of grief.

I always thought that when someone died, you suffered the one big grief of losing that person. But it isn't that way at all. A death brings not just one big grief but lots of smaller ones.

Not long ago, Dad and I stood in front of the display of Valentine cards knowing that for the first time in fifty-seven years, he couldn't give his beloved anything for Valentine's Day. He could hardly see the display for his tears. When our daughters have something to celebrate—a missing tooth or a good grade on a test—I want them to be able to call her. I see Mom's teapots and suddenly realize she won't be having any more tea parties with our daughters. We are grieving hundreds of small losses stretched out over time—a card that can't be given, a call that can't be made, the tea parties that won't be celebrated. We grieve each one.

The Underwear Saga

One of Dad's biggest challenges is learning to keep up with all of the little things that Mom used to do for him. I am daily astonished by what he doesn't know. Lately we have been living with the underwear saga.

My father tells me that his underwear is sagging. In seventy-nine years he has never bought his own underwear. He wants to know what he is supposed to do now that his underwear is sagging. How saggy does your underwear need to be before you get rid of it? Where do you buy new underwear? What do you do with your old saggy underwear after you buy new underwear? This is what we talk about each day. Sagging underwear. I swear to you, I am not making this up.

He wanted to know exactly how many pairs of underwear he should have. I told him he could have as many pairs of underwear as his heart desired. That was not good enough. He decided to count the pairs of underwear that Mom had kept in his drawer, write down the number (twelve), and always try to keep that same number.

My mother always told us, "If I go first, your Dad is going to need your help." Somehow, I imagined she meant moral support and a listening ear. It never occurred to me that we would be having painstaking discussions about what to do when his underwear sagged.

I should not have been so surprised. Human love and care are made up of little things—like Mom's faithful provision of underwear for Dad and Dad's filling up the gas tank for Mom. When we lose our loved ones, we miss not only love in the abstract but all the little things we did for our loved one and all the little things our loved one did for us.

When Mom and Dad were first married, her father was annoyed that his new son-in-law didn't pick up his clothes off the floor but left them there for Mom to pick up. Years later, when my brother, John, and his new bride, Susan, were returning from their honeymoon, they stopped by to visit our Ridgway grandparents. Our grandfather pulled John aside to give him one piece of advice about married life. "Son, pick up after yourself. Don't leave your drawers lying around on the floor."

When Len and I were newly married, our Grandmother Ridgway cornered me in the kitchen and told me, "Men like to eat. Feed him well. Here's my pound cake recipe." I was terribly disappointed by their advice and, frankly, astonished that after fifty-plus years of marriage they couldn't do any better than that.

Now, having been married almost three decades, I'm thinking that was pretty good advice. Pick up after yourself and make lots of pound cake. That's the sort of thing marriages and other relationships are made of. If you love somebody, it gets played out in the smallest ways.

Grief Decreases Productivity and Increases Accidents

My house is a mess. I can't find anything. On top of that, I just wrecked our car.

I am so far behind at work, I don't think I will ever catch up. I'm just not as productive as I ordinarily would be.

It turns out that I am not alone. According to a nationwide study in 2003, employee productivity decreases markedly following the death of a family member. The annual cost of that decreased productivity was over $37 billion. Eighty-five percent of managers said that their decision making was poorer in the wake of a family member's death; 90 percent of blue-collar employees noticed decreased concentration and increased mistakes and injuries.[6]

I can only think of one upside to this trend. When people grieve, they tend to think about decreased productivity differently than they might otherwise. Even though productivity is down, perhaps they have the happy good fortune of not caring. In the face of grief, people can't get quite as worked up about decreased productivity. It's like reading Ecclesiastes multiple times a day for months on end. It changes your point of view. The Gross Domestic Product is down? So what? Vanity of vanities. I didn't get a raise this year? Oh, well. Vanity of vanities. I wrecked my car? All is vanity. All is vapor. It is all fleeting.

The Vortex Effect

As she grieved for her dead husband, Joan Didion noticed triggers—like passing by her husband's favorite restaurant—that would bring back an overwhelming sequence of memories and feelings of grief. Throughout the book she writes about this "vortex effect" and recounts the memories that followed. Didion would drive many miles out of her way to avoid places that held a lot of memories.[7]

Lists of common grieving behaviors often include this tendency to avoid places and things linked with the dead. In the days after Mom's death, we tended to avoid anything associated with those last difficult weeks in the hospital. Dad didn't go back to the hospital until several months after Mom's death. I still find it very difficult to listen to the instrumental piano hymns we played in Mom's room those last weeks. It makes me sick to my stomach to hear that beautiful music. In fact, I swore I would never listen to piano music again. It's not working out so well for me. You may not have noticed, but pianos are everywhere. You cannot escape them. I speak from experience.

Even in the extremely unlikely event that I could avoid pianos, I cannot avoid all the memories from that hard time in the hospital. We might as well try to hold back the sea using only the power of our will. The waves keep rolling on.

Taking a Break from Grief

I've had it with grief. I'm tired of Mom being dead. This is getting old. I never knew that grief was so tedious. Can I please do something else now?

I get it now. Mom's dead. She isn't coming back. We have to get on with things. So, let's do that. Let's put this grief stuff aside and get on with it.

I always thought the bereaved were supposed to confront their emotions and not avoid the difficulties of grief. But it turns out that a fair measure of avoidance can be just fine. There is a new grief therapy called the "dual process" model that even recommends it.[8] Researchers noticed that people often grieve in an oscillating pattern: facing the difficult emotions of loss and then avoiding the emotions by doing something else for a while. They decided to call this temporary avoidance not pathology but a healthy coping behavior.

When people describe grief they often use the image of waves. I googled "waves of grief" and found 54,800 web pages from which to choose. The image of waves makes sense to me. Sometimes waves are tsunami-like; we can't do much, if anything, about them. At other times, we have some choice in how we respond.

As a girl I loved to dive into the ocean waves. I quickly learned that my experience of a wave depended in large part on my response to it. I had a choice; I could "let go" to the wave and be carried where it took me, or I could fight it and get knocked around. Either way was intense, but giving in to the wave and riding it out was clearly the better option. I never had control of the waves, but I usually had some say about how I would respond.

I have thought a lot about that image—the waves of grief—and wondered how I might stop fighting those waves and, instead, ride them out. Only now does it occur to me that I have tended to focus on the waves of grief and not on the troughs between the waves. When I was wave riding, I learned that I had a choice, not only about what I would do when the waves came but also what I would do between the waves. I could worry about what was going to happen when the next big one came, or I could use the time to relax my body and take a few deep breaths.

Here I am in the middle of grief. I cannot control the waves, but I can choose how I will respond to them when they come and what I will do between the times. I can move with the wave of grief as best I can, and when it ebbs, I can seek out things that are healing for my family and for me.

Finding Comfort and Hope in the Landscape of Grief

The terrain of grief is hard, but we are not without help along the way. As we grieve, it's good to be mindful of what helps us and those we love. We can keep a list, pick a few things, and pledge to do them. I reflect here on what has given our family comfort as we have grieved.

Antidotes to Grief

Grievers are often comforted by many ordinary activities: talking with family and friends, listening to music, and praying. Dad finds solace in his daily mountain walks with his brother and the attention of friends and family. He has also talked with his pastor about his loss. Other family members have seen grief counselors and joined grief groups. Many of these same antidotes to grief are found on lists taken from the Internet and books. The medieval theologian Thomas Aquinas drew up his own five-part list of "remedies of sorrow."[1]

According to Aquinas, grief is lessened, first, by pleasure. Weeping and groaning are also recommended. "Tears and groans" lessen sorrow because "a hurtful thing hurts yet more if we keep it shut up" (Art. 1 and 2).

Aquinas also counsels the sorrowful to seek the sympathy of friends. When friends offer sympathy, the grieving see how much they are loved and this gives them pleasure. Moreover, sorrow is a weight pressing down on the bereaved; sympathetic friends take on a part of the burden (Art. 3).

Prayer of the heart is also a balm for the wounds of sorrow. If pleasure is a remedy for sorrow and if prayer of the heart is the highest pleasure of human life, then, Aquinas reasons, prayer must be a remedy for sorrow (Art. 4).

Aquinas closes his list of remedies with the simple comforts of bathing and sleeping, which help ease sorrow by restoring the body to its "normal state," and this is a source of pleasure: "Therefore, since every pleasure assuages sorrow, sorrow is assuaged by such like bodily remedies" (Art. 5).

If the terrain of grief varies from person to person, the lists of things that would help must vary as well. Aquinas's words have prompted me to make my own list that includes: exercising, spending time outside, being thankful, helping others, being with friends and family, watching movies, reading, praying, making and listening to music, eating good food, taking hot baths, and getting plenty of sleep. If Aquinas is right that "every pleasure assuages sorrow," the list could go on and on.

Thanksgiving Therapy

Dad has taped a few letters to his bathroom mirror, including one from me. In those first days in the hospital, Mom and Dad fell into depression. I should have let them be, but I had the gall to write them a letter advising a self-help program I wanted them to try alongside Mom's physical therapy. I called it "Thanksgiving Therapy," and it included seven exercises, all of which they had mastered years before.

- Thankfulness
- Hugging
- Adoration (worship and prayer)
- Nature
- Keeping it positive
- Singing
- Giving

On reflection, I see that as their life was falling apart, pushing them to "keep it positive" was probably not the most compassionate response. I think *asinine* is the word I'm looking for. But today, seeing the list on Dad's mirror, I realize that the therapy I recommended for Mom and Dad *then* would be a good antidote for my grief *now*.

Thankfulness and Praise

When Mom and Dad were in a funk in those terrible early days in the hospital, the first thing that disappeared was praise. In a normal person, this might not be strange, but praising God is Dad's refrain. If someone were to follow Dad around with a recording device on an average day, she or he would surely discover that the phrase Dad utters most often would be "praise God!" followed closely in second place by "Oh, s_ _ _!"

In those early weeks in the hospital the cussing was outstripping the praising. I should have left them alone in their misery, but we were trying to encourage them to be positive because we thought it might increase Mom's chances of survival. As the first step of their Thanksgiving Therapy, I gave them this exercise— in writing:

> Thankfulness and praise of God have been the therapy of choice throughout the Christian church. Please find three things a day for which you can give thanks to God out loud in each other's presence. You guys are masters at this one. You can do this therapy and still cuss about fifty things that go wrong. This is not to discourage cussing and moaning but just to encourage the addition of more praise and thanksgiving.

The first day Dad thanked God that he and Mom had six good children (the three originals plus spouses). The next day, fed up with us, Dad thanked God that he and Mom had no more than six children. Somewhere along the way, in spite of my meddling instructions, they started praising God again.

It took me a long time to realize that praising God might be a good idea for me too. Frankly, this advice seemed absurd and even heartless at first. I have not been in much of a mood for praising. But I'm making the effort. Why not? Maybe praising God and being thankful generally would be an appropriate response to grief—almost a liturgical response, and certainly a healing response. It's worth a try.

When I'm overcome by sadness, I stop and repeat, as long as it takes, "Thank you God for our mother. Thank you. Thank you." And then I cuss a little too—just for the hell of it.

Martin Prechtel, a writer from a Pueblo tribe in New Mexico who lived in a small community in Guatemala for several years, claims that "the Mayan concept of grief and praise come from the same word. Grief is thought of as praise for what we have lost. . . . Our grief is our praise; they awaken in each other's arms."[2]

If grief and praise "awaken in each other's arms," it's no surprise that Dad and many others would find praise to be a fitting response to their grief. I have been thinking not only about the Mayans but also about the Calvinists and the Wesleyans. The Westminster Confession poses the question: What is the purpose or end of human life, the end for which God created us? According to Calvinists, the "correct" answer is "to glorify God and to enjoy him forever." And glorifying God means praising and adoring God. If God created us for praise, it makes sense that it would be a fitting response throughout our lives—including in our grief.

Speaking in Dublin to a crowd of Irish Methodists, an elderly John Wesley asked this same question: What is the one end or purpose for which God created us? Wesley's answer was: "You are made to be happy in God." As soon as children begin to talk, parents should tell them "many times in a day . . . 'He made you; and he made you to be happy in him; and nothing else can make you happy.' . . . Indeed, this should be pressed on every human creature, young and old" (§§ 10-11).[3] Our happiness can be summarized, Wesley preached, in "two words, gratitude and benevolence; gratitude to our Creator and supreme Benefactor, and benevolence to our fellow creatures" (§16).

Recent studies of happiness confirm Wesley's claim. Happy people tend, among other things, to be grateful and altruistic. Psychologist Robert Emmons writes, "Grateful people experience higher levels of positive emotions such as joy, enthusiasm, love, happiness, and optimism, and . . . the practice of gratitude as a discipline protects a person from the destructive impulses of envy, resentment, greed, and bitterness."[4]

I am working hard on gratitude and praise, but some days cussing just seems like a better fit. There are moments when instead of following Emmons's advice to give thanks, I would just as soon throw his blasted book clear across the room.

Helping Others

For Wesley, not only gratitude, but also benevolence, is essential to human happiness. Recent studies have confirmed Wesley's second claim. Altruism, like gratitude, is good for people.[5]

As my parents grew older, one of their chief desires was that they would be able to continue helping others. They loved nothing better. The day of my mother's funeral was hard on all of us, especially my father. By nightfall, he was unsteady on his feet and was finding it hard to walk. He grew confused and asked, "Where is JoAnn?" Then he remembered. He had never looked so old, so lost.

Dad was in bed in his pajamas while most of the family walked down the hill to the lake below my parents' house. Suddenly one of his grandsons, Duvey, came charging down the hill. A truck and car had just collided on the highway right in front of Dad's house. We all knew that Dad would rush to help. Len and our brother-in-law, Marc, took off running up the hill. Sure enough, Dad was in the highway. He had stopped both lanes of traffic and pulled a truck wheel off the road. He helped the driver climb out of his truck and limp to the shoulder. Now Dad was standing in the middle of the road directing traffic in his baby blue flannel pajamas.

Our elderly father, who just minutes before had seemed so beaten, was suddenly euphoric. He was glowing. He had the strength of a much younger man and was a commanding presence standing there on the highway in the dark, signaling cars to stop and to go. It was a tonic for his grief. Even on the day of his wife's funeral—especially on the day of his wife's funeral—our bereaved father wanted to do his part to save the world.

Grief and Prayer

The fourth-century Christian ascetic Evagrius drew up a list of eight things that tempt a person away from prayer. Grief was among them, along with gluttony, lust, avarice, anger, listlessness, vainglory, and pride—not a promising roll call. Evagrius's eight were amended and became, over time, the standard list of "seven deadly sins." For Evagrius and many others, grief was countered by its opposite: joy. He described grief as an obstacle to prayer; joy, by contrast, nurtured prayer.

Remembering the saddest moments of Mom's illness and our grief, I am struck by the growing awareness that grief and sorrow have not been a hindrance to prayer. If anything, grief and sorrow appear to be an opening to prayer and consolation. "Blessed are those who mourn, for they shall be comforted." Grief has driven us to prayer and worship, and prayer and worship have offered solace in our grief.

Our mostly Protestant family also includes Roman Catholics, Hindus, and Jews. I can't help noticing that many Protestant churches, including my own, do not have the rich patterns of communal worship and prayer to mark later stages of grief beyond the funeral and burial. Because my sister and her family are Jewish, we United Methodists quickly learned what we were missing, and together we improvised. In the Jewish tradition, there is a ritual to mark the setting of the gravestone. As we stood around Mom's gravestone, we read traditional Jewish prayers, sang some of mom's favorite hymns, and threw in a few extemporaneous prayers for good measure. When my sister and her household marked the one-year anniversary of Mom's death with a *yahrzeit* observance around their dining room table, we joined them over the Internet by Skype. We lit candles and drank our mother's favorite tea while reading Scripture and watching Anna and Katherine eat massive amounts of brightly colored candy. I suspect that our mixing and invention of traditions would not satisfy all Jews or all United Methodists, but it satisfied us. We learned that we needed rituals to mark our grief and the passage of time. In the absence of shared traditions, we made do with what we had, and we made up what we did not have! It worked for us.

Grief and Touch

Our Grandfather Ridgway often told us what he missed the most after his wife's death; he longed for her touch. In his last years he moved to a retirement center near my parents' home and began going to their church. My father passed the word that my grandfather loved hugs, and soon people literally lined up at his pew to hug him. He loved it.

Toward the end, his mind was going; he woke up each morning with no idea what day of the week it was. Because he loved his Sunday hugs, he would go ahead and put on his Sunday clothes, just in case. Mom had found him a blue-and-white-striped seersucker suit like the one he had worn when he and our grandmother eloped in 1928. Every morning, there he would be, sitting in the lobby, dressed in his seersucker suit with a fedora on his lap. He wanted to be ready in case the church van came by. Six days out of seven, somebody would come by the lobby to tell him, "Sorry, Mel, it's not Sunday." He would respond, "Well, I was just hoping." After his wife's death, more than anything he wanted to be touched.

Katherine has noticed the therapeutic effect of touch. When she sees that I am sad, she tells me, "Mama, you need a hug."

When she hugs me, I can feel a difference in my body. I relax and breathe more deeply. My body feels lighter.

This is not a trick of my imagination. Hugs and other kinds of good touch can have profound effects on the body. They can lower blood pressure, decrease stress hormones, foster happiness, and increase oxytocin, sometimes called "the love hormone." Even athletic performance may be enhanced by touch. A group of scientists studied fist bumps, high fives, and chest slams of players in the National Basketball Association and discovered that teams and players who touched more tended to have better performance on the basketball court.[6]

Christians should not be surprised to learn that touch can be therapeutic. Throughout the Gospels, Jesus reaches out his hand to touch people. Jesus touches the eyes of the blind man in Matthew 9:28. When he meets up with a deaf man who has a speech impediment, Jesus sticks his fingers in the man's ears, spits, and touches the man's tongue. What does Jesus do when he sees that Peter, James, and John, shocked by the appearance of the long-dead Elijah and Moses, have fallen to the ground in fear? He comes and touches them.

When Mom and Dad were so depressed in those early days in the hospital I recommended hugs as a part of their therapy, but they never had to be reminded. They couldn't help themselves. This became a problem when the doctors told us that Mom was at high risk for infections and we should limit touch. We tried to stop Dad, but it was futile. He would slip into her room when no one was around, so they could engage in surreptitious, forbidden hugging. In retrospect, I'm glad they were noncompliant; it was the best thing for them. Now, without Mom around, the thing he longs for most is her touch.

Grief and Singing

Under the happy influence of morphine, Mom came up with some entertaining ideas in those first weeks in the hospital. She told us, for example, that her doctors were requiring her to sing before she could go home. She would say to us commandingly, "Now let's all sing together, so I can get my life back. Let's sing me out of this place." She would start singing, usually the old hymns "Love, Mercy, and Grace" and "Standing on the Promises." We would all sing, not that we had much choice. If we weren't sufficiently loud or enthusiastic, she would stop her singing and encourage us. "Come on now, everybody, sing. 'Twas Love that gave at greatest cost. A life that mine should not be lost.' "

I realized long after that it wasn't her doctor who recommended singing therapy; it was me. I included singing in their Thanksgiving Therapy and wrote to them: "Singing can decrease pain and improve blood pressure, heart rate, and depression. As the days progress, please aim for fifteen minutes of singing a day."

The research is compelling. Singing has been linked with higher levels of endorphins and oxytocin, lower blood pressure, a stronger immune system, and improved lung function and mood.[7] Because of these benefits, music therapists use singing as a therapy for many illnesses. Singing has even been recommended as a therapy for grief.[8]

Martin Luther often praised singing and gave his highest praise to music: "I plainly judge . . . that except for theology there is no art that could be put on the same level with music, since except for theology [music] alone produces what otherwise only theology can do, namely a calm and joyful disposition."[9] Frankly, as much as I love theology, if it's a calm and joyful disposition that I'm looking for, I'll choose singing.

With Mom gone, singing links us together and with her. At family gatherings, our mother always had us get out the songbooks. In the old days we sang to please our mother; now we sing to console ourselves.

Nature and Grief

Grief and good weather have driven me outdoors. I carried my laptop to a hammock hung over a small creek behind our house. To rock the hammock, I dip my foot in the cool water, only a few inches deep, and push off from the rocks. Two woodpeckers, a downy and a red-bellied, work the sycamore trees above me. Even their hammering and the sounds of the creek become a piece of the stillness surrounding me. In nature, grief is overtaken by calm; it isn't taken away but simply held and absorbed.

In the weeks following her mother's death in the spring of 1951, our Grandmother Ridgway wrote letters to her sister Laura about the long walks she and our grandfather took through the woods near their home in Forrest City, Arkansas. Along the top of Crowley's Ridge, they saw woodpeckers and robins caring for their young. They found sweet williams and azaleas growing wild. On their next walk, they carried a shovel and burlap sacks; they dug up the plants and carried them back home to transplant in the beds around the pecan trees in their backyard. Being outdoors and caught up in the world of nature—not just as a spectator, but as an engaged participant—brought our grandmother solace.

What is so healing about pecan trees, red-bellied woodpeckers, and sweet williams? What happens in nature that doesn't happen as readily in human-made environments?

When Henry David Thoreau was twenty-five, he lost his older brother, John. Thoreau wrote a letter to a friend reflecting on nature's equilibrium in the face of his brother's death: "Soon the ice will melt, and the blackbirds sing along the river which he frequented, as pleasantly as ever. The same ever-lasting serenity will appear in this face of God." At the close of the letter he mentioned a young neighbor, recently dead: Waldo, the son of Ralph Waldo Emerson: "Neither will nature manifest any sorrow at his death, but soon the note of the lark will be heard down in the meadow, and fresh dandelions will spring from the old stocks where he plucked them last summer."[10]

Erazim Kohak, a Czech philosopher, turns to the ancient Latin phrase *vis medicatrix naturae*, meaning "the healing power of nature."[11] Spending time in the woods and under the stars does not take the pain away but, instead, shifts a person's point of view. When humans are surrounded only by objects of their own making, they are easily deluded, coming to see themselves as the "center of the universe" and their grief and pain as "an event of cosmic significance." In natural settings the human is not the center of the world "but a dweller within it." When humans "discern the humility of their place in the vastness of God's creation, then that creation and its God can share the pain. . . . That healing power then is no longer the *vis medicatrix naturae*. It is the *vis medicatrix Dei*." The healing power of nature is subsumed within the healing power of God.

Dad spoke recently at the Hot Springs botanic gardens for their annual "blessing of the blossoms" ceremony—a time to ask God's blessing on the trees and flowers of the garden. Dad told me, "They asked me to bless the blooms, but I told folks that the blooms bless us. They reveal the nature of God. They offer a sense of awe and utter gratitude. They plow through the despair of our lives. We don't bless the gardens. The gardens bless us."

How do gardens bless us? What is it about azaleas and pecan trees that make them a source of blessing in grief? Perhaps it isn't so much nature's indifference to human pain that blesses us but its radiance with divine life.

The azaleas and the pecan trees bless us because in them God's glory is revealed. In the novel *Gilead*, the Reverend John Ames reflects on his approaching death and the beauty of the world he will soon leave behind.

> It has seemed to me sometimes as though the Lord breathes on this poor gray ember of Creation and it turns to radiance—for a moment or a year or the span of a life. . . . . Wherever you turn your eyes the world can shine like transfiguration. You don't have to bring a thing to it except a little willingness to see.[12]

In the wake of ecstatic religious experiences, many people report that their eyes open to the radiance of creation. Indeed, this is one of the most common features of mystical experiences across religious traditions. Several years ago, after a series of these experiences, I journaled about the luminosity of nature:

> I went outside . . . and was stunned . . . by the beauty and aliveness of the birds' bodies—especially a chickadee that kept coming within a few feet of me and then a large woodpecker— a red-bellied. . . . I watched the woodpecker for the better part of an hour and was overcome by its glowing beauty. . . . The trees shimmered. The entire world was radiant.

On these rare occasions, I am left with the impression that the world not only *looks* luminous but also actually is luminous. I would swear that all living things are radiant with God's presence.

This radiance may explain why in grief and pain we seek the "common bush," the sweet william, the red-bellied woodpeckers, the lark, the stars. If these living things are luminous with God's presence, it is no wonder they offer us comfort in grief. Not only do they remind us, as Kohak insists, of the small place of our life and grief in the universe but also they prompt us to remember our eternal significance as luminous living things made from dust and the breath of God: "Creation . . . turns to radiance. . . . You don't have to bring a thing to it except a little willingness to see."

Grief and Pleasure

Mom and Dad's anniversary just passed—their fifty-seventh and Dad's first without Mom. Dad retold the story of the weekend they were married: the $40 he had saved up to pay for tuxedos and a honeymoon; the speeding ticket that left him only $25; the sycamore tree he and Mom's little brother, Mel, climbed the night before the wedding; the sight of my mother in her wedding dress; their honeymoon at his annual Methodist preachers' meeting in Hot Springs. He smiled and laughed as he talked, and all the while tears were sliding down his face.

Grief stands in sharp contrast to other negative emotions—ordinary depression for example—because it can hold together feelings that appear to be at odds: sorrow and joy, regret and gratitude, pain and pleasure. One of the classic marks distinguishing grief from depression is the capacity to feel pleasure. People who are severely depressed, on the one hand, generally experience anhedonia—or the absence of pleasure. The bereaved, on the other hand, are typically still able to enjoy ordinary pleasures. Our bereaved father savors his strawberry milk shakes, his morning walks with his brother, Warren, pork roast made by his sister, Joy, and happy memories of his sweetheart.

The recent psychiatric diagnosticians were not the first to observe the presence of pleasure within grief. The Japanese, for example, have an ancient word—*airaku*—that means grief and pleasure combined.

Edmund Burke, the eighteenth-century philosopher, noted the link between grief and pleasure: "The person who grieves, [lets his grief] grow upon him; he indulges it, he loves it." The attraction of grief is rooted in the love one bears for the object of grief—the deceased. Deep grief always embodies deep love: "It is the nature of grief to keep its object perpetually in its eye, to present it in its most pleasurable views . . . to go back to every particular enjoyment, to dwell upon each . . . ; in grief, the pleasure is still uppermost."[13]

As Dad tells of their courtship and wedding, pleasure and sadness are intermingled. After finishing the story, he said through tears, "I am the happiest man that ever was. I never changed my mind from the beginning to the end. I am the luckiest man in the world."

Grief and Laughter

Dad finally admitted to me this morning that his new underwear—the first underwear he has ever bought for himself—was, he learned belatedly, made for tall men. At five foot five Dad is not tall; the underwear came up to his ribs. He thought this was a great joke.

Dad and Mom were usually laughing about something—most often a joke on themselves. One evening several years ago I called their house, knowing that they should have come in that afternoon from a long trip. When they picked up the phone, they couldn't stop laughing, because they had found, on arriving home, that they had no electricity. "Our electricity was cut off! We forgot to pay the bill! Ha ha ha!"

I'm thinking, "That's not funny!" Daughters lose their sense of humor when it comes to the welfare of their older parents. Of course, Mom and Dad thought my consternation was even fun-nier than their electricity being cut off.

In the Christian tradition, laughter has been called a sin by some theologians. The failure to laugh has been called a sin by others. Laugh or don't laugh—either way, somebody is going to call you a sinner.

John Chrysostom wrote, "This world is not a theater in which we can laugh, and we are not assembled in order to burst into peals of laughter but to weep for our sins."[14] With Mom and Dad, laughter wasn't a substitute for weeping over sin. They always had strong consciences that left a great heaviness when they felt they had done something wrong.

When Dad is laughing in the face of difficult situations, he often says, "You gotta laugh, cuss, or cry." But he doesn't laugh instead of cussing and crying; he does all three—sometimes all at once. If anything, I think Dad is laughing more than usual these days. It doesn't seem to be a denial of his pain but a healthy sur-vival skill.

"Hey Bud, Go Find Your Own Butt"

Oddly enough, those terrible days in the hospital were filled with moments of outright hilarity. We got to know a little man who was mother's next-door neighbor that first week in the hos-pital. I don't know what his medical problems were, but from our limited point of view, the chief problem was that he didn't like to wear clothes. He would stand in his doorway in nothing but a dia-per, except for the few times when he forgot the diaper and dis-played himself in all his not-so-glorious form. When we did not see him, we still heard his voice because every few minutes he would yell for the nurses instead of pressing his call button.

One afternoon my brother, uncle, and I were standing in the hall when this gentleman came to the door and asked—loudly— if any of us were nurses. "I need a nurse! Are you a nurse?" My brother explained that we were not nurses and said to the man, "Sir, you need to find your button." The man turned around, bent over, poked his finger at his naked backside, and yelled, "Buddy, I don't need to find my butt. I know where my butt is!"

My brother, like most pastors, has had dozens of hours of mandatory sexual misconduct training and knows not to comment on the butt of anyone to whom he is not married. John stood in the hall saying over and over in a calm voice, "Sir, I am not interested in your butt."

Several nurses hurried over to escort the man back into his room as he yelled, "That boy wants to know where my butt is! I know where my butt is!" He turned back to John and yelled, "Hey, bud, go find your own butt!"

In the hospital and the days following Mom's death, when we wanted to remind one another to mind our own business or when we needed a laugh, all we had to say was, "Hey, bud, go find your own butt!"

Denial and Optimism

Dad's been having a rough time lately, but when I asked him this morning how he was doing, he sang out, "I'm FINE. I'm FINE. Soft and sweet as a baby's beHIND." I said, "Dad, don't be lying." He didn't deny the falsehood; he defended it: "Hell, dar-lin', it's better than saying 'Oh s_ _ _!' all day long."

Dad's grief is often deeper than he lets on. He puts a good spin on things because he wants to save others the pain of seeing his pain and because it's a deeply ingrained habit. Maybe that's all right. Maybe some days it makes sense to say, "I'm fine," and then try to live into that claim.

I read a study on optimism and pessimism. People who were more pessimistic had a more accurate view of reality; their predictions were closer to the mark. The optimists were further off the mark in their predictions, but they tended, overall, to have better outcomes than the pessimists and to be happier and healthier along the way.[15]

Do people who downplay the depth of their grief have better outcomes over time? That seems unlikely; books about grief warn against the dangers of "minimizing grief." But there may be room for a modest portion of denial. Perhaps a little happy avoidance can coexist with healthy grief.

In the last chapter, I mentioned the "dual process" perspective that takes this need for avoidance into account.[16] Grievers are to move back and forth between directly confronting their loss and pain for a time and then avoiding the pain by focusing on other things. It seems that men are especially good at this second prong of the dual process model. One study of older bereaved men found that avoidance and distraction are among their most common coping mechanisms.[17] That explains a lot.

I Don't Always Believe What My Mind Thinks: Reframing Our Loss

One evening Katherine and I were driving through a storm and she was worrying about tornadoes. Next thing I knew, she was explaining why the frequency of tornadoes increases as humidity decreases. Dry weather means more tornadoes; stormy weather means fewer tornadoes. It was a fascinating theory—utterly wrong, but fascinating.

As she was in the middle of this complex description, she began to realize that no matter how scared she was of tornadoes, her theory did not hold up. There was a long pause, and then she concluded: "Mom, I don't always believe what my mind thinks."

That line has stuck with me: "I don't always believe what my mind thinks."

I have remembered it as I have thought about the many things we say to ourselves to make our grief more bearable. "I'm so grateful that she isn't suffering anymore." "She would have been so miserable in a nursing home." Those things are true. But the deeper truth is this: those lines are a way we protect ourselves from the pain of missing her. Oddly enough, even though we know exactly what we are doing, the lines still offer comfort.

Sometimes, after we agree that we are glad Mom is no longer suffering, one of us will even add, "It's poor consolation, but we'll take what we can get." Even with that final stroke of brutal honesty, we are still consoled.

But do I really believe what my mind thinks?

My personal favorite word of consolation comes from the cowboy movies of my childhood. When I am overcome with grief, I often say to myself, "Good for you, Mama. You got the hell out of Dodge." I feel better immediately. The image of our mother wasting away in her hospital bed is replaced by an image that couldn't be any more different: mother in her strength and vigor, choosing to hightail it out of Dodge on a golden palomino, turning to smile and wave at the earthbound residents of Dodge as she rides out of town in glory. If those are the two images from which to choose, it's not hard to guess which one I'm going to favor. But do I really believe what my mind thinks?

The field of cognitive therapy is based on this idea that our patterns of thinking and the ways we talk to ourselves shape our emotional states.[18] Granted, cognitive therapy is usually centered on the task of trying to get rid of distorted thinking and to replace it with something at once more positive and more accurate. But maybe it's not all bad to replace accurate yet depressing thoughts with positive if somewhat more distorted ones. Who doesn't love a good exit scene during which the hero heads off into the sunset? The fact that Mother's exit looked nothing at all like that doesn't make it any less compelling.

But do I really believe what my mind thinks?

Weddings and Graveyards: Looking to the Future and to the Past

Both the past and the future bring us great consolation. The brightest part of the week Mom died was our nephew Trey's engagement to his sweetheart, Kelsea. Trey (a.k.a. John Miles III) had worked out a plan to propose in Hot Springs that weekend. After Mom died, Dad asked Trey if he would mind going ahead and proposing on Friday night—after Mom's burial on Friday but before her memorial service on Saturday. That way we could announce the engagement at Mom's memorial service. Dad loves marriage.

On Friday morning before we left for the cemetery, John Miles I, II, and III swapped stories about how they made the money for engagement rings for their sweethearts. Early Friday evening this beautiful young couple came by the house on their way to Garvan Gardens where Trey planned to propose. We loved being in on the secret. A half dozen family members waited up to find out what had happened. The next day at Mom's memorial service my sister, Deborah, announced their engagement. It was a joy and comfort for everyone—especially Dad—to have this new marriage beginning as Mom and Dad's marriage was ending. We are all suckers for a love story.

Six months later, Trey and Kelsea were married. The reception was held in the church fellowship hall where we had gathered to greet friends and family after Mom's funeral. It was an extraordinary means of grace to hold both of those events together in our minds.

Right after the wedding, Dad, the girls, and I took off on a road trip to some of Dad's childhood haunts, visiting family graves and his home place in south Louisiana. We drove along the Louisiana and Texas coasts and spent the night at an old Galveston hotel where he and his brother, Warren, had stayed with their mother when they were little boys. Dad watched his granddaughters swim in the Gulf, just as his mother had watched him and his brother swimming there seventy years before. Our nephew Josh joined us, and we drove to the presidio at Goliad in south Texas. In 1769 some of our Acadian ancestors overshot their intended destination of New Orleans and shipwrecked on the Texas coast. They were imprisoned in Goliad by Spanish officers and during their six-month stay were put to work on the early construction of the mission there. More than two and a half centuries later, we spent the night in that mission and had it to ourselves. Dad sat for hours under mesquite trees in the enclosure, watching his grandchildren play and thinking about those shipwrecked Acadians who had labored there and about all the generations in between.

Looking both to the future and the past offers great consolation. We see our short lives as they are linked with those who come before and after us. That night at Goliad, we talked about our ancestors long dead and the new household Trey and Kelsea were forming together. Dad told me, "It puts everything in perspective and brings to mind the bonds we share across the generations."

CHAPTER 4

Reintegrating the Dead: Bringing the Dead Along with Us on the Journey

I tried my best in those first months of grief to let go of Mom; I failed miserably. That old advice to "let go" of the dead has been replaced in much grief literature by a recommendation that grievers find ways to reintegrate the dead into their lives. This practice can never take away the pain of loss, but finding a place for the dead in our lives can provide both comfort on the pilgrimage of grief and a fitting way to honor our dead.

Our Relationship with the Dead

Toward the close of her memoir of grief, Joan Didion writes, "If we are to live ourselves, there comes a time when we must relinquish the dead, let them go, keep them dead."[1] On those ubiquitous lists of the stages of grief, letting go is usually near the end of the inventory. Now I wonder if letting go of the dead is all it's cracked up to be. Letting them go and keeping them dead is tough, especially when you don't really want to. Grief expert Tony Walter insists that the bigger challenge is not letting go of the dead but reintegrating them into our lives.[2]

That all sounds fine in theory, but how do we renegotiate a relationship with someone who is not physically present? My mother is dead. Our relationship was built on ordinary things I took for granted—phone calls made, gifts shared, meals jointly prepared and eaten, her smile, her gaze, her voice . . . all now gone. How do we learn to live with the dead, when the ordinary means by which we relate no longer hold?

Walter describes four ways people commonly relate to their dead loved ones in their private lives. First, in several studies of widows and widowers, about half reported they had felt the presence of their dead spouse. Second, Walter notes that many people find a connection with the dead through their religious beliefs—especially an expectation they will be reunited with the dead in eternity. Third, the bereaved talk to the dead. Walter writes that men tend to go to the graveyard to talk, while women most often talk with their dead husbands at home. Fourth, the bereaved often look for places and things that "have a power to evoke a bond with the dead": cemeteries, household shrines, photographs, jewelry, or just about anything linked with the dead.

How else do we reintegrate the dead? We give thanks to God for them. We tend their gravesites. We acknowledge the presence of the saints as we approach the altar for communion. We do acts of charity and justice in their memory. We imitate their virtues and take on their good causes.

As I have searched for ways to reintegrate my mother into my life and our family life, I have been remembering how she and my father kept alive our bonds with the dead. In the hallway of each parsonage, Mom always hung old family photographs, most of them of people who had died before my siblings and I were born. I always liked the one in which the little Martin brothers wore white shirts and ties but no shoes and another of their daddy, years later, preaching on a street corner in Hot Springs, his congregation gathered around, a wooden collection box sitting on a folding stool. On special occasions, we used the quilts they had made. We cooked the favorite recipes of the women and prayed the mealtime prayers of the men. We made regular pilgrimages to graveyards across Acadia Parish in south Louisiana and Woodruff County in east Arkansas. The dead were a living part of our family.

Telling Their Stories

More than anything else, the dead were brought to life for us in the telling of their stories. My parents and other relatives often talked about the dead as we sat around the dinner table. Tales of their failures and victories were our morality plays.

My grandmother often told us about her mother. They lived together in a tiny sharecropper's cabin on the Cache River in Arkansas, many miles from the nearest school. At night my grandmother would hear her mother crying, begging her husband to move closer to town so their children could attend school. They moved when my grandmother was eleven. She finally learned to read and later became a teacher, paying for college by picking cotton in the summers and working as a maid throughout the school year.

Those stories from early in the twentieth century seem far away, and yet they still carry power to shape us. A few months ago, Katherine wrote an application essay for a girls' public school—the Young Women's Leadership Academy in Fort Worth. She told this same story about her great-grandmother and added, "I am a good reader because she worked so hard to learn to read, and then she told her children and her children told their children and they told me that you have to get an education."

My regular lectures about education made little impression on Katherine. It's the story of the dead she remembers—an illiterate girl in a sharecropper's cabin and her mother's tears. Katherine is under the impression that she is a good reader because her great-grandmother struggled to learn. She is surely right. How could I have ever considered letting go of the dead?

Treasured Objects

In grief, people often mark their bond by keeping close at hand a few special things that belonged to the dead. Loved ones will sometimes wear the clothing or jewelry of the deceased. I am now wearing Mom's pink angora sweater and black shoes.

Years ago we became friends with an old man who lived on a fishing boat on a pier in the North Sea. He carried in his wallet a scrap of paper with a short shopping list that his dead mother had drawn up many years before on what turned out to be her last visit to the butcher shop; she died on her way back home. One evening at a pub, he showed it to us after drinking a few too many beers. We could see that he had taken it out of his wallet and unfolded and refolded it many times; it was a ratty treasure. He read the note aloud, "Two lamb chops kidneys," and then put his face in his hands and wept.

New Technologies

New technologies offer new ways to reintegrate the dead into our lives. Facebook pages become temporary memorial sites after a death. Grieving friends leave messages, not only for the family but also for the dead: "We miss you so much!" "Not a day goes by that I don't think about you." Grieving loved ones can chose from many different online services if they wish to set up memorials to their dead; Virtual Heaven, Cyber Memorials, and 1000memories are just a few of the options. The CaringBridge website we created during Mom's illness offered a way for me to write about grief after her death and for friends and family to share in our experiences and offer words of comfort.

Our daughters have found their own ways of staying connected with their grandmother. On their Wii—a popular gaming system they play on our television—they created characters for different family members, including their dead grandmother. These characters show up randomly in their games. Today I was pleased to watch as Mema competed with the girls in a runaway mine train race and a "mole stomping" contest. As Anna told us later, "Mema did pretty good for a dead lady."

"Vehicles in which Our Ancestors Ride"

I have been reading the autobiography of Mary Livermore, a nineteenth-century social reformer. Reflecting on the link between the generations, she writes, "Dr. Oliver Wendell Holmes says, that 'our bodies are vehicles in which our ancestors ride.' And he might have included our souls in this statement, without fear of contradiction."[3] We, body and soul, are "vehicles in which our ancestors ride."

How are we related to our ancestors? We have genetic links with those from whom we are biologically descended. My siblings and I have the long, narrow face that was worn by the Miles and Vickery families of generations before. My Uncle Warren lacks the same piece of cartilage in his left ear that was missing from the ear of his Uncle Bill.

What else do we receive from our ancestors—the ancestors with whom we are linked by DNA or adoption, as well as our ancestors in the spirit? Most of the things we receive are not likely to be as obvious as the shape of an ear, but they are no less real: love for God, passion about education, commitment to family. How do we, in turn, give these things to our children—our children in the flesh and our children in spirit?

A few years ago I was watching Anna and Katherine horse around with two of our nephews, Josh and Caleb, both of whom are more than a decade older than our girls. I had this strange sense of déjà vu; something about their way with kids seemed so familiar. Suddenly it came to me. They were playing with our daughters in the exact way their father had played with them when they were boys: the same intonation, the same mannerisms, even the same words.

All those hours spent with their father, I thought they were just horsing around. It turns out their father, Marc, was forming them to be men who could love children and help shape another generation. What I saw that day was not the biological inheritance from their father but the inheritance of habit and manner. They carry not just a set of genetic traits—the thick dark hair and dark eyes—but a set of habits of working and playing and loving, a way of existing in the world. As they spent time with their father, they had become more and more like him.

That transmission of habit and manner moves not only from parent to child but also from teacher to student, from mentor to follower, from friend to friend, and sometimes from child to parent or from student to teacher. These ways of being in the world are transmitted as surely as a gene for a misshapen ear. Of course, we may be formed in healthy ways or distorted by those around us. The scars can be passed from one generation to the next as surely as a gene for eye color. We have a say, both in how we allow ourselves to be shaped and how we continue to shape others.

Cloud of Witnesses: Seeing Ourselves and Our World Through the Eyes of the Dead

Lorraine Hedtke, a grief counselor, created a series of exercises to help people find "ways to . . . 'keep alive' the relationship with the person who has died." In a recent article, she offers this quotation: "When we see ourselves through the loving eyes of those who have cared for us, our lives are easier to live."[4]

I have been thinking about that phrase "when we see ourselves through the loving eyes of those who have cared for us." On what turned out to be her last Mother's Day, Mom heard her pastor preach about the cloud of witnesses and told the congregation that he often imagined their beloved dead "sitting up in the balcony encouraging us along our way." Mom told us she liked thinking of her parents and sister Gena in worship with her.

When our Aunt Nora Mae went to church as a girl in Crowley, Louisiana, she was surrounded by three pews full of Mileses. Until she died recently at ninety-eight years old, she was still sitting on that same pew in that same Methodist church. All the rest of the Methodist Mileses, except for Aunt Nora Mae and her ninety-seven-year-old sister-in-law, Evelyn, had gone on long before. But, even so, she didn't think of her pew as empty. She told us, "Every Sunday, my pew is full!"

I once saw that pew on a Sunday morning, and it did not look full. But if Hebrews 12 is to be believed, maybe her pew stayed full after all: "Therefore, since we are surrounded by so great a cloud of witnesses, let us also lay aside every weight and sin that clings so closely, and let us run with perseverance the race that is set before us, looking to Jesus the pioneer and perfecter of our faith" (vv. 1-2).

Our continuing bonds with the dead make sense in the light of Christian understandings of this "cloud of witnesses." What difference might a cloud of witnesses make in the way we live? John Calvin noted that while these witnesses had previously been "associates in the same race," now they are not in the place of "rivals, seeking to snatch from us the prize," but their role instead is to "applaud and hail our victory."[5] The faithful dead become our encouragers.

I like to think of Mom in the stands—just as she always was whenever we had a game as children—and she, along with all the other saints, is eager to see us run. They see the best in all of us and are as generous in their view of the race as the best of parents. Of course, we don't know how the saints see things. But absent any evidence to the contrary, I'm going to go ahead and hope that's how it really is. It makes me want to run and to take on the harder task of looking at the race and all the other runners with their encouraging eyes.

"In Eternity This World Will Be . . . the Ballad They Sing in the Streets"

I am still wondering how things might look from the viewpoint of the faithful dead—not just how the dead look upon us, but also how they might see the entirety of the life they left behind.

Might the ordinary preoccupations and pleasures of this life seem less compelling from the point of view of eternity? Or might they take on even greater significance?

Driving back and forth between Hot Springs and our home in Fort Worth while Mom was in the hospital, I listened to the novel *Gilead*. The narrator, knowing he will soon die, wonders how the fragile beauty of this mortal life will appear from the perspective of eternity:

> I can't believe that, when we have all been changed and put on incorruptibility, we will forget our fantastic condition of mortality and impermanence. . . . In eternity this world will be Troy, I believe, and all that has passed here will be the epic of the universe, the ballad they sing in the streets. Because I don't imagine any reality putting this one in the shade entirely.[6]

Might the dead look fondly not only on us but also on our imperfect, broken world? Might the most ordinary moments of this mortal life be, in eternity, the "ballad they sing in the streets"?

Our great-grandmother, Carrie Ridgway, is known to our family by a single story. When our grandfather was born in December 1906, his mother began to hemorrhage. Medical care was poor in that part of rural Arkansas at the turn of the century, and they lived many miles from the nearest hospital. She knew she was dying. After kissing her older children good-bye, she asked to hold her newborn son. She uncovered him and, like new mothers the world over, she examined each part of his body. By the time she worked down to his feet, she had begun to cry. As her sister came to take her baby son away, she put his toes to her lips and whispered, "Oh! How I'll miss these precious little feet!"

What might Mom be missing? Probably Dad with his blue eyes. Over the years, Mom told Dad a thousand times that she liked to see him in blue; it brought out the color in his eyes. It was a rare day when Dad did not wear a blue shirt to the hospital.

Mom crashed several times during those seven weeks in the hospital. In one of the worse of those moments, the doctors had just revived her and the techs were preparing her for emergency surgery. They were trying to keep her awake and told her to focus on their faces and then, "Focus on my eyes, Mrs. Miles." Mom came out of the fog just long enough to whisper, "My husband's eyes. . . . My husband's eyes." Dad drew close to her, and she kept her face on his face, her eyes on his eyes. Those were the last words she ever spoke to him.

When the dead look on their mortal life and their loved ones who live still, might it be an infant's feet that they long for, a mother's soft cheek, or a husband's eyes? Perhaps the ordinary life of the flesh is what the dead miss. That is the "epic of the universe, the ballad they sing in the streets."

The fourteenth-century German mystic Meister Eckhart wrote about the pleasure God takes in pouring Godself into every creature. God enters our mortal life, not with sorrow or uneasiness, but with delight: "It is just as enjoyable for [God] as when someone lets a horse run loose on a meadow. . . . Such is the horse's nature that it pours itself out with all its might in jumping about the meadow. This it would find delightful; such is its nature."[7]

God comes into the world, not just in sorrow to save humans from their sin, but also in joy to participate in the good life of the flesh, to know the pleasures that come from the caress of a mother's hand or a glimpse into the eyes of the beloved. My husband's eyes.

Heaven

Heaven has been on Dad's mind lately. He told me the other day, "I look forward to seeing all my people, most of all JoAnn." As we anticipate our reunion with the dead, we find another way to connect with them; they not only are a part of our past but become a part of our future as well.

In a sermon written not long before his own death, John Wesley reflected on the topic of heaven; the sermon reads like the notes of a man eager for his next great adventure.[8] Like my father and many others, Wesley insisted that we would recognize our loved ones in heaven and continue our intimate bonds with them. The universal love we will feel in eternity for all creatures will not lessen the "peculiar affection which God himself implants for our relations, friends, and benefactors" (§11).

Wesley also speculated about what heaven might look like. As his ordinary senses were failing, he wondered what it would be like when he got to heaven and his spiritual senses were fully opened:

> In a short time I am to quit this tenement of clay. . . . When my eyes no longer transmit the rays of light, how will the naked spirit see? . . . What astonishing scenes will discover themselves to our newly-opening senses! . . . Above all, the moment we step into eternity, shall we not feel ourselves swallowed up of Him who is in this and every place, — who filleth heaven and earth? (§§ 2–7)

Since Mom's death, I have often thought about what it will be like in glory. We anticipate our coming fellowship not only with our beloved dead but also with the One who is in this and every place—who filleth heaven and earth.

Of course, if you think about it carefully, the prospect of an eternal family reunion is not entirely pleasant. As I was extolling its joys, a family member reminded me of its shortcomings:

> Tell me, why is this such a comforting idea? Let's be honest; we have a hard time being at family reunions for more than three days! Have you ever thought about how veeerrry long eternity is? And think about this: We would be in the company not only of our parents and aunts and uncles and their parents and aunts and uncles but also their grandparents and on and on back for generations. And eventually we would have our children there, plus nieces and nephews and grandchildren and on and on. It's hard enough taking care of fifteen or twenty relatives at one time; what if we had fifteen or twenty generations to look after? What about one hundred generations or more! Who's going to cook for all those people? You and me, that's who!

I haven't worked out all those details yet, and I suppose I don't have to. Surely, I can count on at least a little help from the One "who is in this and every place" and from our dear mother, of course.

"We Could Not See [the Chariot], but We Felt the Fire"

Early Methodist ideas about death and heaven were shaped in part by stories about the dying. It was common among early Methodists and other pietists for the faithful to gather around the deathbed, not only to encourage the dying but also to be encouraged by them. As John Wesley printed deathbed stories in his *Arminian Magazine*, a whole genre of storytelling arose to describe the final hours of the dying.[9]

Even today, if you talk to hospice chaplains and nurses, most will tell you stories about deathbed visions (referred to affectionately in the hospice literature as DBVs, for short). It seems that the dying often "see" or have long conversations with dead family members. Seeing or talking to a dead family member or friend is one of the most common features of DBVs around the world.

I have been reading the autobiography of Laura Haviland, a nineteenth-century Quaker turned Methodist, who was an abolitionist and a worker on the Underground Railroad before the Civil War. When Haviland was a young mother with eight children, her husband and youngest child both fell ill with a strep infection and died. Soon afterward, her mother died of the same illness, and a week later, Haviland's father, still in deep grief for his wife, became ill too. His family gathered around his bed as he was dying; he blessed them and gave witness to his faith. Haviland wrote, "His last words, almost with his last breath, were, 'Here she comes.' "[10] I like to think that when Dad dies, he might at the end catch a glimpse of our mother, and whisper, "Here she comes."

I grew up thinking it was a rare thing to experience the dead; I could not have been more wrong. The bereaved, as well as the dying, often report seeing their dead loved ones, hearing their voices, and feeling their presence. They sometimes smell the scent of their cigars or a favorite perfume. I have heard Mom's voice twice, felt her presence several times, and had very vivid and comforting dreams about her.

It is tempting to argue about whether or not these experiences are real, but that is a question we cannot answer. We *do* know, however, that these experiences are real to those who have them and that they often appear to be beneficial. In several studies, the bereaved reported that these experiences were a comfort and helped them find healing in their grief.[11]

Jarena Lee, a nineteenth-century holiness preacher from the African Methodist Episcopal Church, described in her autobiography the death of her friend, Mrs. Simpson, who was surrounded at the last by family and friends, including Lee. They prayed together around the bed, and everyone sang hymns, including a final song requested by Mrs. Simpson, "O for a Thousand Tongues to Sing." Lee wrote, "As we sang . . . she raised herself up in bed, clapped her hands and cried: 'He sets the prisoners free! Glory! Glory! I am free! They have come for me!' She pointed toward the east. . . . 'Don't you see the chariot and horses? Glory! . . .' She dropped back upon her pillow, and was gone. . . . 'we could not see [the chariot], but we felt the fire.' "[12]

We know little about eternity and the life shared by the dead. But perhaps at the deaths of our near ones—at the death itself and in the days following—the veil is thin and we receive an impression of what they experience, a sort of secondhand glimpse of eternity. We do not see the chariot, but we feel the fire.

Finding Hope, Moral Purpose, and Spiritual Transformation in the Landscape of Grief

We cannot change the circumstances that led to the death of our loved one. We cannot turn the grief away. But we can choose how we will respond to grief. The pilgrimage of grief can make us better people and bring us closer to God. Through this experience, we can find ways to help others and make a better world. The good that emerges after a death does not undo the loss. It does not make what happened right. Still, in spite of it all, this hard thing can bring many gifts.

But there is another side to grief. Sometimes grief, especially unresolved grief, brings not gifts but destruction. It can ruin our closest relationships, drive us to addictions, and wreck our faith. Grief can destroy the things most dear to us, but it does not have to. We have some choice in how our grief shapes our lives and the lives of others. Learning to grieve well matters.

What Is the Use of Grief?

W hen they were old men, John Adams and Thomas Jefferson wrote letters to each other: letters touching on many subjects—including grief. In 1816, Jefferson wrote to Adams wondering about the purpose of grief and its role in "the perfection of the moral character": "I have often wondered for what good end the sensations of Grief could be intended. . . . What is the use of grief."[1] In his reply, Adams called to mind the portraits of great people in whose faces one sees "strong traits of pain." "These furrows," wrote Adams, "were all ploughed in the countenance by grief." Why did those who had grieved deeply often make the best legislators and magistrates? Because, Adams insisted, grief shapes moral character. The bereaved are

> compelled by their grief. . . to review their own conduct toward the deceased, to correct any errors or faults in their future conduct . . . to recollect the virtues of their lost friends, and resolve to imitate them. Grief drives [humans] into habits of serious reflection, sharpens the understanding, and softens the heart.[2]

Can we humans know, Adams then asked, why these losses come upon us? No, that knowledge is beyond our finite human vision: "We poor mortals have nothing to do with it, but to *fabricate all the good we can out of all inevitable evils.*"[3]

The Other Side of Grief

Adams may have been right that legislative bodies and courts are often peopled and led by those who have known much grief. But let's be honest, so are meth houses and prisons. It's commonplace to note that addictions and other serious problems can often be traced back to unresolved grief.

Grief can be a source of healing and transformation, but it can also be the seed ground for addictions and mistrust. It can blow holes in marriages and destroy friendships. It can ruin lives. But it does not have to. We have some choice about what we will make of our grief.

I feel bad about saying this to anyone who is already hurt-ing, but it has to be said eventually. However hard the loss, however much we hurt, we have decisions to make. And they matter. They matter to us and they matter to the people around us.

We need to choose well and keep choosing well. We need to develop habits of prayer and healthy living. We need to take care of ourselves and those we love. We need to surround ourselves with people who will support us and help us choose well.

Deuteronomy has to be one of the most boring books of all time, but it does have a few memorable lines including this one: "I have set before you life and death, blessings and curses. Choose life so that you and your descendants may live" (30:19).

In theory anyway, this is a fairly clear choice. Right? Who wouldn't prefer blessings over curses? But if you are anything like me, you may have a mixed record when it comes to choosing life and blessings. It's the strangest thing. There are days when I run as hard as I can right past the blessings and into the embrace of the curses.

I've decided to think of my record on the blessings/curses option as if it were a batting average. If you get a hit once in every three times up to bat, you are doing great. You just have to keep showing up at bat, watching the ball, and swinging when the time is right.

When we are in grief, choosing blessings over curses can be hard. It takes attention to what we are feeling and what's going on around us. It takes an intentional commitment to do whatever work needs to be done to keep ourselves healthy and headed in the right direction. Grief is not something that just happens to us. We shape our response to grief. And our choices matter.

Meaning-Making Animals

> We who lived in concentration camps can remember the men
> who walked through the huts comforting others, giving away
> their last piece of bread. They . . . offer sufficient proof that
> everything can be taken from a man [or woman] but one thing,
> the last of human freedoms—to choose one's attitude in any
> given set of circumstances—to choose one's own way.[4]

Viktor Frankl, psychologist and Holocaust survivor, insisted
that humans are "meaning-making" animals. In horrible circumstances, even in a concentration camp, one may still retain the
capacity to interpret and respond, "to choose one's own way."

This human impulse to interpret and respond is at the heart of
the pilgrimage of grief. In interviews with grievers, researchers
noticed that over time most people began to think about the
meaning of their loss and grief.[5] They looked for ways to
bring good from bad. They reflected on how they were being
transformed.

The researchers noticed that this habit of "meaning-making"
not only was *common* among grievers but also appeared to be good
for them. In several studies, the bereaved who could *not* find
meaning in their loss or discern benefits emerging from it, had
more severe problems with their grief; their grief was more likely
to be maladaptive or detrimental. They suffered from more health
and emotional problems and had a harder time moving back into
ordinary activities and relationships.[6] Meaning-making did not
make the grief go away or make the death right, but it did help the
grievers live better lives and find joy in the midst of pain.

Meaning-making often has an ethical component.[7] Grievers
take on causes and virtues of their dead. They grow in compassion. They seek ways to help others who are hurting. They
become advocates. A group of mothers whose children had been

killed by drunk drivers started MADD, Mothers Against Drunk Driving; they created a revolution that changed how people in the United States think about drunk driving and that led to legal reform and saved thousands of lives.

For many grievers, their capacity to find meaning in loss is linked with religion and spirituality.[8] Some believers come to question their faith after the death of a loved one, and they begin to think differently about God. For others, beliefs about and experiences of God give them hope not only for the dead but also for the living—for themselves and their families. Grievers often report that their faith in God helps them keep going and finding ways to help others.

I have been struck both by the ways that faith has helped in our grief and by the ways that it has not. Faith may comfort us in our sorrow, but it does not save us from it. In fact, faith may do just the opposite—instead of erasing our suffering, faith appears to compound it, and that compounded suffering, however difficult, can itself become a source of many gifts.

Faith Doesn't Take Away Grief; It Breaks Open Our Hearts

When we were with Mom at the hospital, we looked forward to the nightly prayers read over the hospital intercom. Every few nights, we heard Reinhold Niebuhr's serenity prayer: "God grant me the serenity to accept the things I cannot change, the courage to change the things I can, and the wisdom to know the difference." Some nights this prayer gave me comfort, and other nights prayer for serenity in the face of things we cannot change seemed just flat wrong. Wouldn't serenity in the face of the ruin of my mother's health be not faithfulness but betrayal?

At the hospital and in the months following Mom's death, I made heroic, if utterly ineffective, efforts to live as if I were a person shaped by the serenity prayer. Honestly, I was not even doing a credible imitation. At best, I was "resigned" to accept the things I could not change, but there was nothing serene about it. Frankly, I was nine large parts p_ _ _ed off and one tiny part serene.

As an old man living with the aftereffects of a series of strokes, Niebuhr grew sick at heart about his famous serenity prayer.[9] He was uneasy about the acclaim he was receiving for the prayer because he was no longer able to live up to it. When he wrote the prayer, he was young and healthy; it wasn't so hard to accept the things he couldn't change when life didn't need much changing. After the stroke, accepting the things he couldn't change was nearly an impossible challenge. He wrote:

> [The letters] embarrassed me because I knew that my present state of anxiety defied the petition of this prayer. I confessed my embarrassment to our family physician, who had a sense of humor touched with gentle cynicism. "Don't worry," he said, "Doctors and preachers are not expected to practice what they preach." I had to be content with this minimal consolation.[10]

Okay, perhaps preachers are not always expected to "practice what they preach." But if the faith they proclaim in good times offers little consolation in bad, what value is it? What use are all our prayers if they aren't more help when we really need them?

Soon after Mom's death, Dad reminded me of a passage from 2 Corinthians 5:7. He told me, "'We walk by faith, not by sight.' We can't know where this road is going, but faith carries us on."

Faith does carry us on. Even so, I have to confess that I've been struck not only by what faith does but also by what it does not do. I would have thought that faith would make grief easier. The pain that comes with grief doesn't seem any lighter for those who believe than for those who don't believe. Sure, I'm comforted by the assurance that Mom lives still. I'm given solace by the promise of God's presence through all our suffering. But that promise and all the other assurances of faith don't make me miss her one small bit less.

Maybe I'm wrong, but if anything, faith makes things more difficult not less. Now that I think about it, I don't know why I was expecting that faith would mean less pain and fewer heartaches. Christianity is all about broken hearts. The very world God creates ends up breaking God's heart. We can't even get through chapter three of Genesis before God is in mourning. And when God comes into this broken world in Christ, God is broken by it.

I am sorry to say that our broken God does not let us off the hook. If we make even a feeble attempt to imitate God and to love others, we are going to end up broken. Why was I expecting that faith would make my heart hurt less in grief? Faith and love break our hearts. Grief is just one more hammer blow in the breaking.

But God does not leave us broken; God uses all of our life, including our brokenness, to bring healing. That's what the incarnation was all about; God uses Christ's embodied life, including his brokenness and death, to heal the world. A few steps from Mom's hospital room was a statue of Jesus with his chest cracked open revealing a swollen, bright red, bloody heart. How horrible! How fitting!

A recent sermon to the new graduates of a divinity school centered on broken and bleeding hearts:

> Over and again, the world's religious traditions speak of the preciousness and power of the broken heart. The Aztecs called it *tlazotli noyol*, "precious, perforated, bleeding heart," without which the sun could not even rise one day. . . . The psalmist reminds God that even if He turns in disdain from burnt

offerings and elaborate sacrifices, He cannot ignore a broken and contrite heart. . . . Paradoxically, we achieve true whole-ness only by embracing our fragility and sometimes our bro-kenness. . . . Life did not intend for us to be inviolable, but to be used for fodder for its workings. We are meant to be chewed up and digested and transformed into the blood and sinews of the world.[11]

What a lousy evangelism slogan: "You are meant to be chewed up and digested and transformed into the blood and sinews of the world." Oh yeah, sign me up.

But that is exactly what I signed up for—or rather what my parents signed me up for—at baptism. Maybe that is what we were all signed up for even at birth. Could we renege on this agreement? Of course, we could try; it is up to us. But in the end, we would not want to. The main thing is not the brokenness and the chewing but the transformation of the world—of all creation, including ourselves.

Tikkun olam is a Hebrew phrase meaning "to repair the world." Through ordinary faithfulness—from praying and keeping the Sabbath to doing acts of justice and going about one's daily work—a person participates in the repair of the world. That is the calling of all faithful people.

When Mom was in the hospital, she dictated this message: "Dear Friends and Family, I am simply overwhelmed by all of your messages of hope and the future. It has been my goal all along to make some contribution to that future, and while it may be more difficult now, I hope to continue along that path."

There Mom is, stretched out in the hospital bed, wires running in and out of her body, and she is thinking not about how the ill-ness will affect her personal future but, instead, about its effect on her future participation in the repair of the world. By God—and by God's grace—she was still planning to make her "contribution

80

to that future." If she could no longer make a difference as a healthy person, she was determined to make a difference by means of her suffering and even her death.

As I have thought about the brokenheartedness we all share, I have come to realize that the main thing is not our brokenness but, instead, what God can make of it. Here, faith does make things better. I may not like the pain, but I know God is making something new of our broken hearts and of a broken world. God repairs a torn world by means of broken hearts, including, and especially, God's own heart.

None of this makes the grief any less painful. But when we trust that God is with us in the middle of it all and is working in the pain to repair the world—including our little parts of the world—we are able to go forward in faith even when we cannot see the path. As my father reminded me, " 'We walk by faith and not by sight.' We don't know where this road is going, but faith carries us on."

Eating Dill Pickles in Paradise: Making Sense of Our Regrets

> Make the most of your regrets. Never smother your sorrow, but tend and cherish it, till it comes to have a separate and integral interest. To regret deeply is to live afresh.
>
> —Henry David Thoreau

After the death of her husband, Reinhold, in 1971, Ursula Niebuhr wrote a series of letters to him as a way to express her regrets. Her husband had often mentioned how much he liked dill pickles from a barrel. After his death she regretted having "failed to pander" to his love of pickles. He also liked cheese and would tell his wife, "In Holland, they often have cheese for breakfast." Ursula Niebuhr wrote, "Why did it never occur to me to give you cheese for breakfast? . . . my sense of guilt remains, for I should have . . . made available not just cheese, but all sorts of cheeses for breakfast."[12]

I suppose I should be thankful that our regrets are often about small things like dill pickles and cheese. That's the case for me. I'm not sure we should have buried Mom in my black boots. They weren't her style. And even though I cut her fingernails that last week in the hospital, I never got around to cutting her toenails. But then I think: oh, for goodness sake, Miles, get a grip. A pedicure and stylish shoes are not high on the list of things a woman might need in her grave.

Here's another regret: why didn't I make her favorite foods more often? Soon before she went into the hospital, I bought a package to make tiramisu, hoping it might tempt her to eat. I didn't get around to it, and then suddenly we were rushing her to the hospital, and she never came home. While she was in the hospital, I kept looking at that box and thinking, "When Mom gets home, we'll eat tiramisu."

We normally think of regret in negative terms, but maybe it's a gift. Thoreau wrote, "Make the most of your regrets. Never smother your sorrow, but tend and cherish it, till it comes to have a separate and integral interest. To regret deeply is to live afresh."[13]

What does that mean? How could regret be a gift? How could it possibly help us "live afresh"? Maybe regrets reflect not so much our failure but a commendable desire to do more than we are capable of doing. Regrets often emerge when there are two good things before us, and we cannot do both of them because we are finite human beings. In this sense, regret can be a virtue.[14]

When her mother was in the hospital dying, my mother wanted to be at her bedside in Little Rock, and, at the same time, she wanted to be at a meeting in Dallas to help prepare to elect a woman bishop. She couldn't do both, so she chose to go to Dallas one night and then hurry home to be with her mother. Her mother died the day after she got back, and for years she was filled with guilt about that one-day absence.

When we were cleaning my mother's desk, we found a letter she had written six months after her own mother's death. The letter was addressed to her mother, and it closed with a litany of the many things she regretted. Mom included a repeated refrain after each regret: "Oh, Mother, please, please forgive me." I look at that list and see not things for which she needed forgiveness but only the inevitable tensions of a rich life with multiple commitments within the church and across four generations of our family.

Regrets often reflect a virtuous desire to do more good things than we are capable of doing. Our drive for the good hits up against the limits of our bodies and our families, and the limits of time and space. If we cared less, we would regret less. And if we were able to do all the good things we wanted to do, we would not be the finite humans God created us to be. Still, I wish I had made that tiramisu.

Ursula Niebuhr concluded her letter,

> Sometimes very pious admirers of yours tell me how sure they are that you are in heaven—and if not sitting at the right hand of God, at least comfortably ensconced. I find it quite difficult to suppress my impulse to say, "Yes, I am sure he is eating cheese and dill pickles." But why not? . . . I like to think of you as, if not seated on a cloud and playing a harp, at least eating cheese and dill pickles.[15]

For the full fifty-six years of their married life, my parents had a running disagreement about a critical theological question: Will there be sex in heaven? They also discussed the companion question: Will there be food in heaven? There was no argument about that one: How could it be heaven without good food?

I am hanging on to the possibility that I will still have a chance to sit down with Mom and share a massive portion of tiramisu. And if Dad is regretting, as I am sure he is, that he and Mom did not get in a little more loving before she died, he can keep hope alive.

The Anti-Serenity Prayer

Upon reflection, I do have a few big regrets. I evidently prefer to think about little things like tiramisu and toenails and repress the bigger ones. Granted, some of my regrets are about things that are the inevitable results of human finitude. I cannot be everywhere doing everything for everyone.

But there are things I did not do that I could have done. Even now, there are things I did not do that still might be done. I deeply regret that my mother did not get better medical care in the months before she became so ill. It is too late now to change what happened to Mom, but it is not too late to do something about the bigger problems.

My mother died because we have put up with a health-care system that provides unparalleled care for the most prosperous among us and shoddy care for the less privileged. As she lived, Mom argued for a more just health-care system; and, as she was dying, she not only continued arguing, but also tried her hardest to draw us into the health-care fight as her proxies.

Arkansas has the lowest payout in the country for Medicare, and fewer doctors are accepting Medicare patients. When my parents' doctor moved away, they discovered it was extremely difficult to find another, even though they had supplemental insurance. My mother called a dozen offices, some within their medical system and some outside of it, looking for a primary care doctor, but to no avail.

At first, the absence of a primary care physician was no big problem. Mom was healthy. She out-hiked her children and grandchildren while on a trip to the Rockies in the summer. But she developed an intestinal virus that went too long untreated. Months went by without the supervision of a primary care physician or a visit to a specialist. By the time she had a colonoscopy, the walls of her colon had thinned. Dad and I took her for a colonoscopy on an early December morning, and before nightfall she was deathly ill. We rushed her to the hospital where we learned that the colonoscopy had torn her colon wall. Emergency surgery followed. It was all downhill from there. Fifty-three days of hell, and then she died. She never stood a chance.

Somewhere in the middle of the various hospital crises, I wrote, "People talk about the ICU experience as a roller coaster. But this is no roller coaster. That image does not touch the horror of it. It's a series of train wrecks, one on top of the other—a train pile-on. Right now we are just praying that there isn't another train coming around the corner; we doubt she could survive one more."

Once the train wrecks started, it became impossible to stop the next one, and the next, and the next. But the whole catastrophe could likely have been avoided if she had had proper medical care from a primary care physician earlier in her illness. All of us together—the pulmonologists, the cardiologists, the neurologists, the surgeons, the nurses, the techs, the physical therapists, and the prayerful friends and family—all of us working well together plus over $300,000 in medical costs could not do in December and January what one primary care physician might have done with ease, efficiency, and very little cost early in the fall: restore our precious mother to health.

My father dubbed me the Holy Terror, but I was second string. In our household, Mom was the original Holy Terror. Whether fighting in the 1970s for the Equal Rights Amendment or in the 1990s for the election of female and ethnic United Methodist bishops, she was a force, and she remained so to the end. She had long been furious about the health-care system, and her fury rose in those months as she searched for a primary care physician and then lay dying in the hospital. "If we had trouble finding help," she asked me, "what about all those poor people who have no money and no connections? What will become of them?"

Mom never had the serenity to accept the things she could not change, but she certainly had the courage to change the things she could. And if, lying in her hospital bed, she was in no position to change some things, she could, instead of serenely accepting it, enlist her family and friends to go out and do some changing for her. Mom lived an alternate, not-so-serene version of the serenity prayer: "God grant me the courage to change the things I can, the persuasiveness to convince others to change the things I cannot, and the wisdom to know the difference. To hell with serenity."

Taking on the Virtues and Causes of the Dead

Grieving people often respond to their loss by taking on the virtues and causes of the dead. Dad is sending checks to Mom's left-leaning group. Our daughters refuse to shop at a national chain that Mom boycotted because of its unfair employment practices. It isn't all about social causes. Lately, Katherine has been looking through a cookbook Mom gave her and planning meals, and I have developed a deep desire for domestic order; those things mattered to Mom.

After his brother's sudden death, Henry David Thoreau reflected on the inspiration provided by the dead:

> Even the death of Friends will inspire us as much as their lives. They will leave consolation to the mourners, as the rich leave money to defray the expenses of their funerals, and their memories will be incrusted over with sublime and pleasing thoughts, as monuments of other [people] are overgrown with moss; for our Friends have no place in the graveyard.[16]

What do our dead friends and family members leave us—not only in their lives but also in their deaths? What do we make from their legacy?

As I have thought about what I wanted to do with my grief and in my mother's memory, the hardest piece has been discerning a fitting response to the one issue that was on her mind at the end: the inadequacy and injustice of health care in the United States. It is hard, in part, because I have no idea how to make a difference with a problem as big as that. Even with the passage of health-care reform, the challenges are still monumental.

Frankly, there is a deeper hesitation; I have shied away from the health-care issue because to address it head-on means I have to face the fact that my mother did not have to die when she did. Here I am almost two and a half years from her death, and somehow I am still overcome by irrationality. I do not want to talk about health care, because then I would have to admit the very thing that I have known to be true all along and that our mother knew to be true: if she had received better medical care before she reached a crisis, she could have easily lived many more years in good health.

Recently, we have begun to take on some of these issues in a very small way. My sister is organizing an exhibit on health care. John and I were elected to the United Methodist legislative body that makes the laws and writes the official statements of the church, and he was placed on the committee that deals with health-care issues. He and I are working on a draft revision of the United Methodist statement. Do I think these things will make a difference? Probably not much. But still, we have to do our part, however meager, not only for my mother's sake and justice's sake but also for our own sake.

Making Something of Our Grief

When Jefferson inquired about the purpose of grief, Adams responded that it isn't ours to understand why bad things happened but, instead, to make of them "all the good we can." When we humans face hardship, our deepest impulse is often to look for a way to make something of our grief. We tell stories of the dead. We set up online tributes and post pictures on our Facebook pages. We establish memorial funds. We work for causes that were dear to the deceased, and we care for their family members. We craft letters to our family and friends, and sometimes we write books. In the light of their death, we try to make sense both of their lives and of our own.

In the end, we honor our dead and make something of our grief, not simply, or even primarily, by becoming like them and taking on their causes, but by becoming more truly ourselves and listening more carefully for what we are called to do. This requires the discipline of attention—attention not primarily to the life of the dead, but to our own lives. The best memorial for our dead may be to grow into our best selves and to make of ourselves an offering to God and to the world. Our stories and tributes have to be more about us than about them, more about the living than the dead. That is how we honor them.

This book is, more than anything else, an invitation to others who are grieving. If you are grieving, I invite you to reflect on how you are responding to your grief and loss. What are you doing with your grief? Are you paying attention to your suffering and to the God who suffers with you? Are you taking care of yourself and looking for things that are healing for you and those you love? How is your loss shaping your life and the lives of those around you? How might you, by God's grace, be called to respond to your loss and to make something of it? How are you being transformed? How is God working in your life for your healing and the healing of the world?

God's Love Finds Its Way in Our Hearts

All this talk of "making something" of our loss, makes it sound like it is all ours to do. The bigger challenge isn't making something of our grief and suffering but opening ourselves to what God is making in us.

I have a love-hate relationship with Romans 5:3-5. Paul writes, "Suffering produces endurance, and endurance produces character, and character produces hope, and hope does not disappoint us." For years, I thought this Scripture was about bucking up in the face of difficulty. Suffering makes you stronger, and that leads to character and hope, and hope does not disappoint us . . . so suck it up, buddy!

I was wrong. I misread Romans and my own suffering by ignoring verse five. In the face of suffering, why does our hope not disappoint us? Here is Paul's answer: "Because God's love is poured out into our hearts by the power of the Holy Spirit." Our hope isn't found in what we make of our suffering but in what God does within us. God's love, God's very self, is poured out into our hearts. That one reality makes almost anything possible.

Years ago I was an associate pastor at a university chapel, Rockefeller Chapel at the University of Chicago. The place is designed to feel massive—32,000 tons of Indiana limestone pressing down into the earth. I was depressed at the time, and when I walked each day down to my office in the basement, I could feel every pound of that limestone weighing on my shoulders. Homeless people dropped by the church most days and wandered down to my office looking for help. Doing good for others is supposed to be good for you, but it wasn't doing a thing for me. Every story of horror—and there were many—brought me a little lower.

A woman I'll call Ruth often came by. She had suffered terrible abuse as child and then gone on to inflict abuse on her own children who had been taken from her. She had lost the people closest to her, some by death, others by abandonment and abuse. Her life was one loss after another.

Ruth would always ask for a sandwich, but what she wanted most of all was to sit down at my silver Smith Corona electric typewriter. She never paid for anything else but always left a penny or a nickel at the typewriter; this was one thing worth paying for. She would take a piece of thin typing paper and cover it completely—top to bottom, left to right, no margins, single-spaced. I was afraid to look too closely at the paper, figuring it was one long, unremitting expression of horror.

One afternoon Ruth left the paper in the typewriter. In spite of my fears, I walked over to take a look. It was a nightmare on paper. Line after single-spaced line, no punctuation, just three words repeated—"oh my god oh my god oh my god oh my god" All I could think was, "Oh my God."

Then something caught my eye. I looked a little closer and saw that every sixth or seventh line she added a phrase to her sorrowful litany: "oh my god oh my god oh my god oh my god your love finds its way in my heart . . . oh my god oh my god oh my god oh my god your love finds its way in my heart."

In the worst of times and circumstances, when all I can think to say is "Oh my God," I remember Ruth. Her life was a living hell. But even in that hell, even in the terror of those typed pages, she knew, somehow, that God's love was finding its way in her heart. I don't know if that made a difference for Ruth, but it makes all the difference for me.

God doesn't create the hell of our lives, but God is with us throughout all of it, working with us and in us to help something good emerge from the worst of circumstances. That is the ground of our hope. God will offer comfort in our sorrow and refashion our lives more and more into God's image. God will help bring us through the holy ground of grief, into something new, accomplishing "far more than we could ever ask or imagine."

We have this hope, not because of something we do or make of our grief, but because of what God does in us. We hope not in our abilities to be strong but in the spirit's power to transform our hearts and lives. No matter what, we can say, with Paul: our hope will not disappoint us, because God's love is poured out in our hearts by the power of the Holy Spirit. No matter what, we can say with Ruth: oh my god oh my god oh my god oh my god your love finds its way in our hearts.

Notes

Introduction: Field Notes for the Pilgrimage

1. John Bowlby and Colin Murray Parkes, "Separation and Loss within the Family," in *The Child in His Family*, ed. E. Anthony and C. Koupernik (New York: Wiley, 1970), 197–216; Elisabeth Kübler-Ross, *On Death and Dying* (New York: Macmillan, 1969); Granger Westberg, *Good Grief: A Constructive Approach to the Problem of Loss* (Minneapolis: Fortress Press, 1971); and Elisabeth Kübler-Ross and David Kessler, *On Grief and Grieving: Finding the Meaning of Grief Through the Five Stages of Loss* (New York: Scribner, 2005).

2. For an overview of this shift, see J. W. Rothaupt and K. Becker, "A Literature Review of Western Bereavement Theory," *The Family Journal* 15 (2007): 6–15. See also Robert Neimeyer, "Narrative Strategies in Grief Therapy," *Journal of Constuctivist Psychology* 12 (1999): 65–85; W. Stroebe and M. Stroebe, *Bereavement and Health: The Psychological and Physical Consequences of Partner Loss* (New York: Cambridge University Press, 1987); Dennis Klass, Phyllis Silverman, and Steven Nickman, eds., *Continuing Bonds: New Understandings of Grief* (Washington, D.C.: Taylor & Francis, 1996); and Margaret Stroebe and Henk Schut, "The Dual Process Model of Coping with Bereavement," *Death Studies* 23 (1999): 197–224.

3. This book embodies and illustrates the newer models of grief just as Granger Westberg's classic text *Good Grief* embodied and illustrated that older model. Although drawing on different perspectives, both are written directly to Christians who are grieving.

4. Kübler-Ross and Kessler, *On Grief and Grieving*, 7.

5. Simone Weil, *Waiting for God* (New York: HarperCollins, 2009), 64.

1. Early Days: Wading Through Hell, Catching Glimpses of Glory

1. D. W. Winnicott, *The Child, the Family, and the Outside World* (Hammundsworth, UK: Penguin, 1964), 88.

2. C. S. Lewis, *A Grief Observed* (New York: Bantam, 1976), 38.

3. Joan Didion, *The Year of Magical Thinking* (New York: A. A. Knopf, 2005), 190 and 227.

4. Dewi Rees, *Death and Bereavement* (London: Whurr, 1997); Julie Parker, "Extraordinary Experiences of the Bereaved and Adaptive Outcomes of Grief," *Omega: Journal of Death and Dying* 51 (August 2005): 257–83; and Nadine Nowatzki and Ruth Kalischuk, "Post-Death Encounters," *Omega: Journal of Death and Dying* 59 (2009): 91–111.

5. *A Grief Observed*, 86.

6. Ralph Waldo Emerson, *The Heart of Emerson's Journals*, ed. Bliss Perry (Cambridge: Riverside Press, 1926), 173.

7. Henri Troyat, *Tolstoy* (Garden City, N.Y.: Doubleday, 1967), 152.

8. *A Grief Observed*, 61–62.

9. See for example, Thomas Reynolds, *Vulnerable Communion: A Theology of Disability and Hospitality* (Grand Rapids: Brazos Press, 2008).

10. Andrew Holleran, *Grief* (New York: Hyperion, 2006), 18.

11. Augustine, *Basic Writings of Augustine*, vol. 2, *City of God*, Book 22:19 (Kila, Mont.: Kessinger Publishing, 2006), 640. See also Beth Felker Jones, *Marks of His Wounds: Gender Politics and Bodily Resurrection* (Oxford: Oxford University Press, 2007).

2. Making Our Way Through Rough Terrain

1. Anthony Trollope, *The Prime Minister* (New York: Harper and Brothers, 1876), 242–43.

2. Joyce Poole, *Coming of Age with Elephants* (New York: Hyperion 1997), 90.

3. See Marc Bekoff, *The Emotional Lives of Animals* (Novato, Calif.: New World, 2007), 14.

4. John Archer, *The Nature of Grief: The Evolution and Psychology of Reactions to Loss* (London: Routledge, 1999).

5. Colin Murray Parkes, *Bereavement: Studies of Grief in Adult Life* (London: Tavistock, 1972), 4.

6. John James and Russell Friedman, *The Grief Index: The "Hidden" Annual Costs of Grief in America's Workplace* (Sherman Oaks, Calif.: Grief Recovery Institute and Educational Foundation, 2003).

7. Joan Didion, *The Year of Magical Thinking* (New York: A. A. Knopf, 2005), 107–13.

8. Margaret Stroebe and Henk Schut, "The Dual Process Model of Coping with Bereavement," *Death Studies* 23 (1999).

3. Finding Comfort and Hope in the Landscape of Grief

1. Thomas Aquinas, "Of the Remedies of Sorrow or Pain," *Summa Theologiae* I–II, q38, a. 1–5.

2. Martin Prechtel, *On Grief and Praise*, compact disc, Flowering Mountain, 1997.

3. Sermon 120, "The Unity of Divine Being," *Sermons* IV, vol. 4, *The Bicentennial Edition of The Works of John Wesley*, ed. Albert Outler (Nashville: Abingdon, 1987), 64–66, §§ 10–11 and §16.

4. Robert Emmons, *Thanks: How the New Science of Gratitude Can Make You Happier* (Boston: Houghton Mifflin Harcourt, 2007), 11.

5. Stephen Post, *The Hidden Gifts of Helping* (San Francisco: Jossey-Bass, 2011) and *Unlimited Love: Altruism, Compassion, and Service* (Philadelphia: Templeton Foundation, 2003).

6. Michael Kraus, Cassy Huang, and Dacher Keltner, "Tactile Communication, Cooperation and Performance: An Ethological Study of the National Basketball Association," *Emotion* 10 (October 2010): 745–49; and Benedict Carey, "Evidence That Little Touches Do Mean So Much," *New York Times*, February 23, 2010, D5.

7. Christina Grape et al., "Does Singing Promote Well-Being?" *Integrative Physiological & Behavioral Science* 38 (January–March 2003): 65–75.

8. William Hoy, "When You Counsel Grieving People," *Grief Connections* 6 (July 2010); and Donna Davenport, *Singing Mother Home: A Psychologist's Journey Through Anticipatory Grief* (Denton, Tex.: University of North Texas Press, 2003).

9. Letter to Ludwig Senfl (October 4, 1530) in Timothy Wengert, *The Pastoral Luther* (Grand Rapids: Eerdmans, 2009), 271.

10. "Letter to Mrs. Lucy Brown" (March 2, 1842) in *The Writings of Henry David Thoreau*, vol. 4, *Familiar Letters*, ed. F. B. Sandborn (Boston: Houghton Mifflin, 1906), 41–42.

11. Erazim Kohak, *The Embers and the Stars: A Philosophical Inquiry into the Moral Sense of Nature* (Chicago: University of Chicago Press, 1987), 42–45.

12. Marilynne Robinson, *Gilead* (New York: Farrar, Straus and Giroux, 2004), 289.

13. Edmund Burke, "Joy and Grief," in *A Philosophical Inquiry into the Origin of Our Ideas of the Sublime and Beautiful* (London: Dodsley, 1767), 54–56.

14. John Chrysostom, Homily VI, Matthew 2:1–2, *Homilies on Matthew*.

15. Martin Seligman, *Learned Optimism* (New York: Vintage Books, 2006).

16. Margaret Stroebe and Henk Schut, "The Dual Process Model of Coping with Bereavement," *Death Studies* 23 (1999).

17. T. R. Fitzpatrick et al., "Leisure Activities, Stress, and Health Among Bereaved and Non-bereaved Elderly Men," *Omega* 43 (2001): 217–45.

18. For more on cognitive therapy and bereavement, see Ruth Malkinson, "Cognitive-Behavioral Therapy of Grief," *Research on Social Work Practice* 11 (November 2001): 671–98; and Neimeyer et al., "Meaning Reconstruction in Later Life: Toward a Cognitive-Constructivist Approach to Grief Therapy," in *Handbook of Behavioral and Cognitive Therapies with Older Adults*, eds. Dolores Gallagher-Thompson, Ann Steffen, Larry Thompson (New York: Springer Verlag, 2008), 264-77.

4. Reintegrating the Dead: Bringing the Dead Along with Us on the Journey

1. Joan Didion, *The Year of Magical Thinking* (New York: A. A. Knopf, 2005), 226.

2. Tony Walter, *On Bereavement: The Culture of Grief* (Philadelphia: Open University Press, 1999), chap. 3.

3. Mary Livermore, "The Battle of Life," in *The Story of My Life* (Hartford, Conn.: Worthington and Co., 1897), 682.

4. Lorraine Hedtke, "The Origami of Remembering," *The International Journal of Narrative Therapy and Community Work* 4 (2003): 58. Quoting Jane Lester and Barbara Wingard, *Telling Our Stories in Ways That Make Us Stronger* (Adelaide: Dulwich Centre Publications, 2001), 43.

5. *Calvin's Bible Commentaries: Hebrews*, trans. John King (Edinburgh: Calvin Translation Society, 1847), 261.

6. Marilynne Robinson, *Gilead* (New York: Farrar, Straus and Giroux, 2004), 66.

7. Bernard McGinn, ed., *Meister Eckhart: Teacher and Preacher* (New York: Paulist Press, 1986), 269.

8. Sermon 132, "On Faith," *Sermons IV*, vol. 4, *The Bicentennial Edition of The Works of John Wesley*, ed. Albert Outler (Nashville: Abingdon, 1987),188–93, 195–97.

9. See, Richard Bell, "'Our People Die Well': Deathbed Scenes in Methodist Magazines in Eighteenth-Century Britain," *Mortality: Promoting the Interdisciplinary Study of Mortality and Dying* 10 (August 2005): 210–23.

10. Laura Haviland, *A Woman's Life-work* (Salen, N.H.: Ayer Publishing, 1984), 46.

11. Julie Parker, "Extraordinary Experiences of the Bereaved and Adaptive Outcomes of Grief," *Omega-journal of Death and Dying* 51, no. 4 (2005): 257-283; and Nadine Nowatzki and Ruth Kalischuk, "Post-Death Encounters: Grieving, Mourning, and Healing," *Omega* 59, no. 2 (2009): 91-111.

12. William Andrews, ed., *Sisters of the Spirit: Three Black Women's Autobiographies of the 19th Century* (Bloomington: Indiana University Press, 1986), 195, my italics.

5. Finding Hope, Moral Purpose, and Spiritual Transformation in the Landscape of Grief

1. "Letter to John Adams," April 8, 1816, *The Adams-Jefferson Letters*, ed. Lester Cappon (Chapel Hill: University of North Carolina Press, 1988), 467, my italics.

2. Ibid.

3. "Letter to Thomas Jefferson," May 6, 1816, *The Adams-Jefferson Letters*, 473, my italics.

4. Viktor Frankl, *Man's Search for Meaning* (Boston: Beacon Press, 2000), 75.

5. Robert Neimeyer et al., "Mourning and Meaning," *American Behavioral Scientist* 46 (2002): 235–51; and Neimeyer, "Searching for the Meaning of Meaning: Grief Therapy and the Process of Reconstruction," *Death Studies* 24 (2000): 541–58.

6. Wendy Lichtenthal et al., "Sense and Significance: A Mixed Methods Examination of Meaning Making after the Loss of One's Child," *Journal of Clinical Psychology* 66 (July 2010): 791–812; and C. G. Davis et al., "Making Sense of Loss and Benefiting from the Experience," *Journal of Personality and Social Psychology* 75 (1998): 561–74.

7. Little has been done on the link between grief and moral formation. The study of "posttraumatic growth" hints at the connections. See R. G. Tedeschi and L. G. Calhoun, "Posttraumatic Growth: Conceptual Foundations and Empirical Evidence," *Psychological Inquiry* 15 (2004): 1–18.

8. David Balk, "Bereavement and Spiritual Change," *Death Studies* 23 (1999): 485–93; and Robert Marrone, "Dying, Mourning, and Spirituality: A Psychological Perspective," *Death Studies* 23 (1999): 495–519.

9. Although authorship of the prayer has been questioned, the best evidence now points to Niebuhr. Laurie Goodstein, "Serenity Prayer Skeptic Now Credits Niebuhr," *New York Times*, November 28, 2009, A11.

10. Reinhold Niebuhr, "A View of Life from the Sidelines," *Christian Century* (December 19–26, 1984): 1195.

11. Kimberley Patten, "When the Wounded Emerge as Healers," *Harvard Divinity School Bulletin* 34 (Winter 2005).

12. Ursula Niebuhr, "Letters to Reinhold: Eating Dill Pickles in Paradise," *Christian Century* 104 (July 29, 1987): 663–64.

13. Thoreau, *The Journal of Henry David Thoreau, (1837–1855)*, eds. B. Torrey and F. Allen (New York: Dover, 1962), 95.

14. The germ for this idea came from Lee Yearley, who wrote about the regret people of one religion sometimes feel when they encounter another religion and can't take it on for themselves. See "New Religious Virtues and the Study of Religion" (paper presented at the Fifteenth Annual University Lecture in Religion, Arizona State University, 1994).

15. Ursula Niebuhr, "Letters to Reinhold: Eating Dill Pickles in Paradise," 664.

16. Henry David Thoreau, *A Week on the Concord and Merrimack Rivers* (Boston: Osgood and Co., 1873), 302.

Made in the USA
Middletown, DE
27 June 2020